ETERNAL MOMENTS

BECAUSE IT ONLY TAKES A MOMENT
TO BE CHANGED FOR ETERNITY

BY: S. R. HENDERSON

CONTENTS

INTRODUCTION

Eternal Moments is the culmination of at least two decades of conversations, observations, and contemplations. I decided to produce this daily devotional to help faith-focused individuals achieve practical application of one Scripture verse per day, every day of the year.

In today's fast-paced world, the constant demands on our lives make it more important than ever to intentionally care for our spiritual well-being, even when time feels scarce. It is my hope that this devotional book will both inspire and attract all who need a daily foundation to support the challenges of each day!

I believe you will be blessed because "It only takes a MOMENT to be changed for ETERNITY!"

JANUARY

January 1

"Therefore, beloved, since you look for these things, be diligent to be found by Him in peace, spotless and blameless" (II Peter 3:14 New American Standard).

Peter is a prime example of a follower of Christ who resigned to place his emphasis on the life to come. Peter knew he was chosen to suffer, so he positioned himself firmly in order to minister to the suffering. Those of you who God has equipped for ministry should examine the burden He has given you. God "usually" takes you through similar trials so you can be effective in helping others. Why would He have you ministering to people you can't relate to? Your compassion will come from familiarity. If you lack compassion in your area of service, you are simply performing Christian charity, trying to score brownie points with God!

I wish I didn't have to put it that way, but we need more laborers and not just workers. Peter calls his audience beloved because God loves them, and he loves them. God knows why you do the things you do, and He will give you His peace when you're genuine. Spotlessness comes from confession of internal struggles; blamelessness is achieved when you guard your conduct. Peter is now mature and completely transformed. Overall, he was a man of great courage who showed normal human weaknesses. Despite his failures, Peter was very dependable and made himself available. God only needs candidates: He will put the "good" into them.

REFLECTION:

January 2

"Then the Lord said to Joshua, 'Do not be afraid because of them, for tomorrow at this time I will deliver all of them slain before Israel; you shall hamstring their horses and burn their chariots with fire'" (Joshua 11:6 New American Standard).

There were many times in Joshua's life where He needed encouragement from God concerning the spirit of fear. I don't think Joshua was timid, but he was probably humble. How would you respond if you were the next leader after someone like Moses? God made it a point to reassure Joshua that he didn't have to "be" Moses in order to follow Him properly. God chose Joshua the same way He chose Moses.

Don't spend your life thinking you have to be anyone else for God to get value from you. You may be His choice to be a great leader. You may be His choice to make a huge discovery, or you may be His choice to just make a profound difference in your household. Whatever the case, you will need courage to do whatever God says. God told Joshua that his enemies would be slain before the battle got really intense. God fights before you do. When you arrive at the battle, the only thing you will have to do is clean up. Sometimes God chooses to prophesy encouragement to you. At other times, He chooses to strengthen your hands. He knows just what you need for every situation.

Face your adversaries with the word of the Lord. Sometimes your adversaries are internal, but the same word defeats them all.

REFLECTION:

January 3

"And unto this people thou shalt say, 'Thus saith the LORD; 'Behold, I set before you the way of life, and the way of death'" (Jeremiah 21:8 King James Version).

Americans have always spoken fondly about freedom of choice. Actually, this is a freedom that humanity has too. Your freedom may not be governmental, but it is certainly a sovereign right. Even those in the constrictions of incarceration have the freedom to choose. The word tells us to choose whom we will serve. God knows that unless love is a choice, it really isn't love. I have spoken to many people through the years who sometimes wonder why God didn't just defeat the devil without us having to go through all these trials.

If evil wasn't an option for us, our choice wouldn't have been authentic. Adam had the option to obey God or disobey God. He chose to disobey, and we have chosen the same. Even after we chose the way of death, the way of life chose us! Love pursued you all of your life. Some of us are still determined to outrun the love of God. This message was to the people of God. It takes a lot for some people to finally "get it." God is very patient, longsuffering, and keeps room for us to turn towards Him. Why wouldn't we choose to live? Why wouldn't we take the road that leads to Him?

It seems like an easy choice, but you should also know that it is the road of affliction. Most of the time the better choice is the more difficult one. It doesn't matter what you go through: it only matters where you end up.

REFLECTION:

January 4

"And the Lord God said, 'The man has now become like one of us, knowing good and evil. He must not be allowed to reach out his hand and take also from the tree of life and eat and live forever'" (Genesis 3:22 New International Version).

The original fall was certainly a fall from grace, but grace didn't fall; man fell! The love of God will always drive Him to do what He needs to do with love as the foundation. God was still gracious in the unfolding of His plan. Your actions will NEVER foil God's plan. Grace may be more accurately defined as: the all-encompassing contingency plan of God.

The arms of grace are always long enough to reach you. The heart of grace is always compassionate enough to find you. The eyes of grace are constantly focused on you, and the God of grace will always establish and comfort you. It would have been a terrible endless tragedy if Adam had been allowed to eat from the tree of life after the fall. He would have been trapped in a deteriorating, aging, and diseased prone body—FOREVER! So, now that God has redeemed and clothed him, the contingency plan of salvation through physical death can be revealed. God doesn't want to sentence you forever in your current state. His actions aren't a reaction to what you did; He knew what you would do, so He unfolds His plan for your restoration.

REFLECTION:

January 5

"[For I always pray] the God of our Lord Jesus Christ, the Father of glory, the He may grant you a spirit of wisdom and revelation—of insight into mysteries and secrets—in the [deep and intimate] knowledge of Him" (Ephesians 1:17 Amplified Bible).

How wonderful it would be to have someone praying for you in this manner. Then, for that someone to be the Apostle Paul! God is the father of glory. He gives permission to radiance and light. He also subdues everything under the power of His will. What is the spirit of wisdom and revelation? When you have a deep, close, personal relationship with God, you get to hear His heartbeat. Everything He calls you to do becomes an earnest expectation. He gives you step-by-step instructions about accomplishing His desires.

Don't misunderstand His steps. He doesn't reveal His instructions in a business-like manner; He reveals them intimately. It would be equivalent to a candlelight dinner as opposed to a board meeting. God will reveal much more to you as you draw nearer to Him. A business setting says, "I don't care who does it as long as it gets done." A candlelight setting says, "Only you can do this for me." The knowledge of God is reserved for His children. A secret can't be figured out; it can only be revealed. A mystery can be solved when you put the facts together properly. Whatever the case, God wants you to know that He would prefer you be in the inner circle.

REFLECTION:

January 6

"So, Abram moved his tents and went to live near the great trees of Mamre at Hebron, where he built an altar to the Lord" (Genesis 13:18 New International Version).

Sometimes the blessings of the Lord will require that you be open to changes. Abram's tents were mobile. After his departure from Lot, God could again lead him. The people in your life at critical points need to be the kinds of people who can "move" with God too. Don't be afraid of new ventures, new alliances, new relationships, and new discoveries.

Whenever something is alive, it always changes. Do things that remind you of what God has said to you. Some people choose to keep a journal; others tell their family members about what God has done. Abram built an altar so he would never forget this turning point in his life. God told him to lift his eyes, look all around, and walk through the land. As you examine your own life, follow those same commands. Let God have your attention, look at what is within your reach, and go get it! Abram was God's man for his generation. I believe God is still raising up people for generational influence. If God is determined to bless you, consider yourself blessed, and walk in humility with His power. Will you be the man or woman who steers your generation?

REFLECTION:

January 7

"Jesus called out to them, 'Come, follow me, and I will show you how to fish for people'" (Mark 1:17 New Living Translation).

There is a transformation in discipleship that only comes when you really follow Jesus. He will use current aspects of your personality, your talents, and your philosophy of life. But He will also mold, shape, remove, and transform other aspects of who you are. He knows that you need to relate to certain types of people. He didn't change the occupation of Peter and Andrew; He changed their preoccupation. We must pay more attention to the plans of God than anything else.

A fisherman is accustomed to using various forms of bait. They're familiar with getting an early start. They know that certain fish swim deeper than others and know what fish to catch in certain seasons and climates. Some people fish for sport while others are professionals. Jesus wants us to become "professional" soul winners. Some days you will catch a lot of fish and some other days you will come home empty.

If you're just fishing for sport, you won't always adjust when you don't catch any fish. If your life depends on it, you can't afford to continually come home empty! Catching the hearts of people is vitally important to your spiritual life, and it promotes the cause of Christ. Spending time with Him will sharpen your skills, broaden your approach, and increase your success! At least with God, the only thing you must do is catch the fish. Let the Spirit of God remove the scales and do the cleaning.

REFLECTION:

January 8

"But rather, you have come to Mount Zion, even to the city of the living God, the heavenly Jerusalem, and to countless multitudes of angels in festal gathering" (Hebrews 12:22 Amplified Bible Classic).

When God visited His people, it was quite an awesome and spectacular occasion. His glory would Iluminate the daytime and eliminate the nighttime. His presence was unmistakable. This is the same God who sends angels as a flame of fire. Even the presence of high-ranking angels would cause humans to shrink n fear. If this is what happens when heavenly citizens visit earth, imagine the splendor where God lives! God has to "confine" the representat on of Himself since the universe is inadequate to contain Him.

I have stood on ocean beaches and been humbled by the vision of endless water. When you stand or the threshold of God's city, expect to be humbled by the vision of endless angels. God made each of them different just like He made each of us different. Mount Sinai caused fear. Mount Zion will cause reverence. The throne of God must have unimaginable beauty. Somehow, I believe because God is alive, and His people are alive, that maybe even His environment is alive and changes constantly. We are accustomed to things remaining the same once they're created. But, when God creates, He gives things the ability to "grow." One thing is for sure; the extent of our imagination will fall far short of God's creativity. Let your mind go crazy with beautiful concepts of colors, gems, and unhindered light. After you're finished, anticipate God exceeding your imagination.

REFLECTION:

January 9

"And most fortunate of all are those who were never born. For they have never seen all the evil that is done in our world" (Ecclesiastes 4:3 New Living Translation).

The presence of evil and the influence of evil can have a profound effect on the outlook of God's people. How can there be fortune for those who were never born? We must remember that the book of Ecclesiastes is a human perspective on life. When you're in the midst of your trials, there is a tendency to think that everyone is in the same boat. Your focus MUST turn from horizontal to vertical. If you constantly look around, you can be easily discouraged. If you find a way to look up, you won't be so easily discouraged.

God tremendously blessed Solomon because his heart was in the right place. Solomon understood the innocent were much better off than those who had been scarred. Evil is running its course in our world, but it will never frustrate the grace of God. The Bible teaches that grace much more abounds wherever sin abounds! That doesn't mean we should give grace something to compete against. It means God has a plan that overrules whatever plans we have. It would be better for us not to see the evil in the world. But, since we have seen the evil in the world, we should take heart in the fact that God has overcome the world. Thank God for the things He has allowed you to experience because He has a specific plan for you.

REFLECTION:

January 10

"Whoever works his land will have plenty of bread, but he who follows worthless pursuits lacks sense" (Proverbs 12:11 English Standard Version).

There is no scripture that supports getting rich quick schemes. God is certainly interested in your prosperity; it will just require your diligence and effort. There is nothing wrong with investing in yourself. If someone wants you to make them profit repeatedly before you make any profit at all, you should investigate much closer before you decide to participate. God has given each of His children access to divine wisdom. We all should have a plan to prosper that God can cooperate with. If you have land, you have a great opportunity to develop equity in your belongings.

God wants us above and not beneath, the head and not the tail, and to be the lender and not the borrower. But you will never be able to lend if you don't own anything! Our biggest problem is the patience to wait for profit margin to increase. Enjoyment later involves sacrifice now. We need self-control to wait for the harvest. Any farmer can tell you how wonderful it is when harvest time comes. But any farmer will also tell you how much work went into the harvest. You must treat the soil, plant the seeds, make sure the seed is watered, pray for plenty of sunlight, and then expect a harvest. How many of God's people expect a harvest but haven't done the necessary pre-harvest work? A "pray only" approach to success is also a worthless pursuit.

REFLECTION:

_____

_____

_____

_____

_____

_____

_____

January 11

"The way of a fool is right in his own eyes, but a wise man is he who listens to counsel" (Proverbs 12:15 New American Standard).

Solomon spent a great deal of time showing us the difference between the wise ones and the foolish ones. This doesn't mean everyone who follows their own instincts is a fool. However, if you refuse good counsel in favor of your own ignorance, you might be "wisdom challenged." In a courtroom, counsel is considered the one who has reviewed your case, examined the evidence, and determined the proper course for your advocacy. God never leaves you without access to godly counsel. Will you listen to it, or will you chart your own course?

The Bible mentions a time when there were no kings in Israel. Everyone did what was right in their own eyes. I know we consider ourselves capable of self-management, but without boundaries, the human heart will resort to chaos and debauchery! It would be permissible to do what you feel if no one was in charge. God is in charge, and we will give account to Him. The people of God have traditionally declined to idolatrous levels when left to themselves. Wisdom will teach you to never do anything important alone. Never make any important decisions alone, and believe it or not, never advise anyone else without seeking God's input. Sometimes we insult God by referring to His counsel as His "opinion." I think an opinion is based on limited knowledge and experience. God doesn't need an opinion. He gives insight into what He already knows! Even if you don't ultimately follow the advice given to you, there is great value in having options to consider.

REFLECTION:

January 12

"For he who said, 'Do not commit adultery,' also said, 'Do not murder.' If you do not commit adultery but do commit murder, you have become a lawbreaker" (James 2:11 New International Version).

I love the book of James because it is straight and to the point. Although there are many categories of punishment for breaking the law, everyone is in the same boat when it comes to breaking God's law. Self-righteousness abounds when a person thinks they are better than someone else because they don't do what that person does. The only time guilt needs a description is for the carrying out of a sentence.

James is telling us that we are all guilty, so don't pretend as though you are "less guilty" than another person because their guilt is more obvious. Since God is the one looking, isn't everyone's guilt equally obvious? It would be the equivalent of getting arrested every time you had an evil thought! The one you will answer to sees everything you do, and He hears everything you think even if you don't say it! Yes, that's right. God is so aware of His universe that even your thoughts resonate to Him. Nothing is invisible to Him. Nothing is intangible to Him. Nothing is disconnected from Him. He gave characteristics to everything in existence. The entire universe is an open display. Jesus is our escape, not our excuse. Our day in court is coming. For your sake, I hope Jesus is your defense attorney. If He isn't, He'll be prosecuting.

REFLECTION:

January 13

"Both hands are skilled in doing evil; the ruler demands gifts, the judge accepts bribes, the powerful dictate what they desire—they all conspire together" (Micah 7:3 New International Version).

According to God's perspective, evil workers are ambidextrous. Very few of us can use each hand equally well. Those bent on mischief give rise to their skill levels tremendously. This state of affairs in Micah's day sounds strikingly familiar to our day. I see nothing wrong with a person earning a living, but when rulers demand gifts to supplement their earnings, it can be a real problem. The part about judges accepting bribes really needs no comment.

Power actually belongs to God, but when He gives power to men, we need to pray for their submission to God's authority. Any one of these power brokers can be dangerous alone, but all together, they present a formidable opponent to righteousness. HOWEVER, no gang or group can withstand the sovereign hand of God. Even every demonic force will meet their doom. Somehow, we must take heart in the plan of God despite the realities of our struggles. It seems God is perfectly content to wait long to vindicate you. The truth is there are things you must come to accept about yourself as well as God. You have the right to question Him when you can fill His shoes.

REFLECTION:

January 14

"I know I am rotten through and through so far as my old sinful nature is concerned. No matter which way I turn, I can't make myself do right. I want to, but I can't" (Romans 7:18 New Living Translation).

Well, there you have t; every Christian's life summed up in a few words. The fact that the Apostle Paul is talking makes us mere mortals feel even more relief. But Paul isn't making this statement to be used as a stamp for disobedience. This is the reai ty of trying to live a victorious life in defeated flesh. Rotten things have a way of taking over no matter how many clean things surround them. The old nature will make you do things you hate, unless you subdue it repeatedly, on a daily basis. Your only hope for doing right is to yield to the Spirit's leading and control. Positive thinking alone won't do it; self-motivation alone won't do it; crying and confession alone won't do it! Everyone is affected by the battle between good and evil. This battle rages internally and externally. I can tell you from experience that even wanting to do right isn't enough! Try to see yourself as someone constantly in desperate need of rescue. God gives grace to the humble. There's nothing wrong with admitting you can't help yourself. Anything you do for God is a process, not a destination. You may have a long string of victories, but you will soon experience defeat. There is a vast difference between experiencing defeat and being defeated! Some things will take a very long time to manage. Even when you manage your flesh very well, don't assume you've arrived.

REFLECTION:

January 15

"Meanwhile, a large crowd of Jews found out that Jesus was there and came, not only because of him but also to see Lazarus, whom he had raised from the dead" (John 12:9 New International Version).

Other scriptures tell us the Jews seek signs, and Greeks seek wisdom. Jesus came as the proof, not to prove Himself! Sometimes God will do something profound in your life that gets the attention of many people. What do you do when God decides to have you deal with celebrity status? I'm sure you think you know how you're going to respond.

Imagine what was going through Lazarus' mind. One day he was DEAD; then he was an overnight sensation. Nothing in the bible tells us how he handled himself. But, he must have been a man of character for Jesus to choose him for the glory of God. Lazarus was still at the table with his family and his Lord. Many of us today would have been out signing autographs and writing books. There's nothing wrong with having a "profitable" testimony. Please be careful to give God the glory. Chances are, if God draws many people to you, He wants you to send them to Him. For some reason, God has always decided to partner with His crowning achievement—man. He figuratively raised you from the dead when He saved you. Many people are watching you, and you don't know it. Stay grounded in your testimony, rooted in His word, and focused on your Savior.

REFLECTION:

January 16

"Peter said to him, 'Lord, why can I not follow you now? I will lay down my life for you'" (John 13:37 English Standard Version).

Peter didn't want to be separated from his Lord at this point. They walked together for several years, and I believe Peter really wanted to see the kingdom of God established in his lifetime. God had a vastly different plan. Peter couldn't go where Jesus was going at that time because He was headed for His cross. Although Peter would ultimately lay down his life for Jesus, he wasn't quite ready yet. This was even before he denied the Lord. We often think we can handle more than what we are currently experiencing. Ironically, we often think we can't handle what we are currently experiencing. Jesus had to prepare Himself to carry the sin of the world. Not only the sin of those living then, but the sin of everyone born in the past, and not yet born in the future. We can't fathom the weight of such a burden. Peter really wanted to be a friend to Jesus, and I appreciate his genuineness. Jesus went places where His followers couldn't go, but you will never go anywhere without Him. At the most difficult transitions in your life, He will be there. He already laid down His life for you.

Following Jesus will take you into many troubling environments. Yet, His strength will be perfected in your weakness. Don't be afraid to be vulnerable in His presence. He knows whether you're REALLY ready to lay down your life.

REFLECTION:

January 17

"Who, contrary to hope, in hope believed, so that he became the father of many nations, according to what was spoken, "So shall your descendants be'" (Romans 4:18 NKJV).

Take the time to examine your life. In order to properly plan ahead, you need to learn from your past. Remember the many times you thought you wouldn't make it? How many times has God snatched you from the claws of despair? Abraham, although he was the man God promised would be the father of many nations, knew what it meant to wonder. Go ahead and admit there were seasons when you wondered if God forgot what He said.

A childless old man becoming a father of many nations is more difficult to pull off than whatever you're facing. The odds are against you; the deck is stacked. Time is running out, and a miracle is your ONLY way out. God is bound by His word to you. It will happen to you too, according to what was spoken. If the word of God can't bring forth fruit in your heart, where else can it grow? I think the most wonderful word in this verse is "became." That tells me it CAME to BE, according to the Sovereign command. Who can nullify the decree of God? His word abides forever! He gives you a more solid foundation than the earth you are standing on. The earth shall fail one day, but His word shall never fail!

REFLECTION:

January 18

"Then Samuel said to all the house of Israel, 'If you are returning to the Lord with all your heart, then put away the foreign gods and the Ashtaroth from among you, and direct your hearts to the Lord, and serve Him only, and He will deliver you out of the hands of the Philistines'" (I Samuel 7:3 Amplified Bible).

This declaration from Samuel came after the Ark of the Covenant was returned to the people of God. It would have been easy for the Israelites to think that things were good because the "symbol" of God's presence was in place. However, Samuel quickly reminded them that deliverance can only be guaranteed by a returning of the heart.

There are many "symbols" today that can make you think God is happy—wealth, power, control, church attendance, good deeds, serving on boards, and more. These are NO indications of the condition of your heart. God is only convinced when you "put away" everything else and serve Him only. We have said for generations that God wants to be the priority. This verse doesn't say He wants priority; this verse says He wants exclusivity. He isn't asking to be the first of many options, and then you can do whatever else you desire. The fundamental problem with God's people has ALWAYS been the tendency to get God's business out of the way, so I can get to mine. That mindset will only yield frustration and disillusion. God has a "Way," and His name is JESUS! He's not merely a symbol of God's presence; He is the Living Word.

REFLECTION:

January 19

"If we believe not, yet he abideth faithful: he cannot deny himself" (II Timothy 2:13 King James Version).

The actions in our lives should be the result of a secure relationship with God. There are things in the previous verses that reveal God's willingness to negotiate with us. However, when we walk in unbelief or fear that God won't have our best interests at heart, He CAN'T negotiate. Have you ever been nervous about the will of God in a particular situation? Sometimes God tests your resolve. Sometimes He tests your courage, and sometimes He just tests your obedience. He doesn't set you up to fail; He sets you up to sail! No matter what happens, He must remain true to His character and His word. He will not deny Himself. The word "abide" is more than just location. Abide also describes the peace of mind you have when submitted to God. When you abide in God, you're not a nervous wreck. When you abide in God, you can rest while waiting for the manifestation of the promise. Your decisions also display ultimate confidence in a favorable outcome. Remember: the things in your life have absolutely no bearing on the divine outcome. God can take the worst of anything and make the best of everything.

REFLECTION:

January 20

"Friend deceives friend, and no one speaks the truth. They have taught their tongues to lie; they weary themselves with sinning" (Jeremiah 9:5 New International Version).

This doesn't sound like a very encouraging passage of scripture, does it? When we know exactly how God sees us, it should help us marvel at His mercy and forgiveness. This is what we are constantly up to in the sight of God. We typically have an inflated viewpoint of ourselves and a deflated viewpoint of God. Every once in a while, God has to show us ourselves so we can come to grips with how bad we need Him. This verse is descriptive of God's people, not pagans. God isn't offended when those who don't know Him oppose Him. What could cause the people of God to be characterized by deception, lies, and pre-meditated sin? When you do something wrong and ignore the inner voice of the Spirit, sin becomes easier. I can't think of many times where people have sinned by accident. If you know right from wrong, there is no excuse for wrong. Yet, God's great mercy is afforded us in the person of Christ. Pardon is granted even though God knows the next time you will offend Him. God's goal is that we get tired of sinning, not tired while sinning.

REFLECTION:

January 21

"When the men had come to Him, they said, 'John the Baptist has sent us to You, saying, 'Are You the Expected One, or do we look for someone else?'" (Luke 7:20 New King James Version).

Well now, even great men have times of discouragement. John gave his life to pave the way for the coming Messiah and still had moments where he wondered if he did the right thing. The ways of God are truly mysterious. We look at the lives of other people and think they can just "snap out of it!" I don't see Jesus sending a message to John that says, "Get a grip."

We typically get a picture for success in our own lives. If you do what God says do, if you go where God says go, if you say what God says say; you should dwell on Easy Street, right? Unfortunately, the answer is a resounding NO! God is more interested in your eternal rewards than your earthly comforts. Isn't your life supposed to be a sacrifice? Whatever you do now is meant to set up your future. We have become creatures of comfort who want our investments to pay immediate dividends. I can't even really believe I'm saying this. I like the same things you do. We all want to know that we haven't totally missed the boat concerning our service to God. Jesus testified that John was still the greatest man born, even though he got discouraged. Before you scold John, imagine how you would feel if you baptized Jesus and later had to sit in a prison waiting to be beheaded because you stood for what's right. John is still a great man.

REFLECTION:

January 22

"And they blessed Rebekah and said to her, 'Our sister, may you increase to thousands upon thousands; may your offspring possess the gates of their enemies'" (Genesis 24:6c New International Version).

This is the end of the story where Abraham's servant went to find a wife for Isaac. Rebekah's family pronounces a blessing on her. This chapter is really a wonderful "type" of "New Testament truth." Abraham's servant is a type of "the Holy Spirit." Abraham is a type of God the Father; Isaac is a type of Jesus. The servant has been sent to a distant land to find a bride for the Father's Son, so Rebekah would be a type of "the church." Even after the servant arrives to get her, the family leaves it up to her to make her own decision.

God won't force you to accept His marriage proposal in Christ. He will speak of His riches, His promises, and His love, and His desire to care for you. As you read the entire chapter, notice how the servant doesn't mention himself or even his name. He only talks about his master and the son. The Spirit doesn't exalt Himself; He only magnifies and exalts Jesus. Finally, the servant gives gifts to Rebekah. God has tremendously gifted you for the status you will have as the bride of Christ. Can the wife of the King of kings be shabby and shameful? He is presently removing your spots and wrinkles preparing you for the wedding night. Even Rebekah's family had enough sense to know she was better off going than staying. Although they weren't poor, they couldn't impede her calling. Therefore, they blessed her as she prepared to depart.

REFLECTION:

January 23

"I look for someone to come and help me, but no one gives me a passing thought! No one will help me; no one cares a bit what happens to me" (Psalms 142:4 New Living Translation).

And you thought YOU were forsaken. We can look at the life of David and see how he had to endure similar things to Jesus. Did you know that you are a type of Christ too? The Bible says He was tempted in the same way you are. That means you are tempted in the same way He was! Your trials will make you feel as though you're the only person on the face of the earth. Everyone else is neck deep in their own issues. The Psalms are full of emotion and the human experience. This song was written when David was hiding in a cave. When you're going through, you look for any sign of compassion, or any sign of accompaniment. It appears as though you can't even buy a friend. The only thing worse than facing the unknown is facing it alone. God's way of bringing you through consists of ordering your steps when no one else is around. Has anyone ever had group surgery? Even in the case of a transplant, one person usually has more at stake than the other. Rarely does anyone want to be tested alone, yet most of us want to be blessed alone. God cares deeply about everything that happens to you. Since He cares, you should probably focus on God and come out of the cave. He loves you too much to dwell in your cave of depression. You must dwell in His world of opportunity. Cry to Him, and He will show you His "Sonshine" that you will NEVER see in your cave.

REFLECTION:

January 24

"But when I stumbled, they gathered in glee; attackers gathered against me when I was unaware. They s andered me without ceasing" (Psalms 35:15 New International Version).

Your enemies always wait until what looks like your weakest point before they attempt to pounce on you. God promises that His strength is made perfect in your weakness, so what looks like weakness to them is just God's way of setting them up. If you think you'll never stumble, think again. You will have plenty of "down" moments as you navigate through this life. But, when you have a relationship with God, those moments won't turn into seasons. No believer should have seasons of depression or seasons of dismay. Prolonged periods of hopelessness are not indicative of those who are still hoping in God. When your hope is in God, it doesn't matter what else is happening. God is eternal; circumstances are temporary. Don't trade in the eternal for the circumstantial. Even if your foes gang up on you, they will still be defeated. If God is for you, who can be against you? People will often plot your downfall, especially if you're doing what they would like to be doing. Your position has been given to you by God, and only God can decide when you should relinquish your crown. Their plotting your downfall doesn't eliminate God's plan for your resurrection.

REFLECTION:

January 25

"Many, O Lord my God, are the wonders you have done. The things you planned for us no one can recount to you; were I to speak and tell of them, they would be too many to declare" (Psalms 40:5 New International Version).

We spend a good amount of time making lists and keeping records of important things in our lives. We make grocery lists, Christmas shopping lists, lists of ingredients for recipes, and "to do" lists. When was the last time you actually tried to list God's wonders in your life? He has kept you in His will; He wakes you every day; He gives you the strength to prosper; He allows you to compete in a land of opportunity; He trusts you with a measure of wealth, and He keeps you from cracking up under intense assault from the enemy! There are many other things worth mentioning if we wanted to continue the list. These are all things that God has planned for you. God's plan for you proves you're not just an afterthought. The fact that you are who you are isn't a surprise to God. Even if you could possibly compile a complete list of God's wonders, there wouldn't be enough time to properly respond to His goodness. The best thing for us to do is think of a few things each day that cause us to marvel at His care. This practice will keep you in tune with Him and draw you into a mode of appreciation. A grateful heart gives God a good field to plant His blessings in.

REFLECTION:

January 26

"Then Jesus was led out into the wilderness by the Holy Spirit to be tempted there by the devil" (Matthew 4:1 New Living Translation).

In the 70's there was a sitcom called "Good Times." In this sitcom, the character Wilona spoke a classic line that I will never forget. She was a single woman who everyone else felt should be attached. She said, "There's a difference between being alone and being lonely." I would also like to add the fact that there's a difference between loneliness and isolation or abandonment. God has promised never to leave nor forsake you. He never promised you would always feel His presence! The first word in this verse is "then." So, when I go back to the previous chapter, I discovered how God spoke from heaven and proclaimed that Jesus is the beloved Son who od is well pleased with. Your greatest tests will come after your greatest victories. The struggles you endure will either break you or confirm that God has great things planned for you. When the tempter came, Jesus was full of the Holy Spirit. When the tempter comes to you, what are you full of? I know we will always have times of victory and times of defeat. Your times of defeat are caused by areas that aren't yielded to the Spirit. Although you might disagree with me, the fact remains that the enemy can only exploit the areas he has power over. I repeat: THE ENEMY CAN ONLY EXPLOIT THE AREAS HE HAS POWER OVER! Although Jesus was alone, He really wasn't by Himself. So, was He really alone? When the Spirit leads you, does He go or does He just point the way for you to go?

REFLECTION:

January 27

"O turn unto me and have mercy upon me; give thy strength unto thy servant and save the son of thine handmaid" (Psalms 86:16 King James Version).

David had a special gift for worshiping God. Although he made grievous mistakes, he was also zealous in seeking forgiveness. I have always admired David's heart for God. Many people will ask, "How could David have a heart for God and do the things he did?" The answer is: the same way you can do the things you do. In addition, we don't find the grace to repent the way David did. Why did David think God was the one who needed to turn? I believe he felt as though God was still chastising him and had turned away from him. There are times in life when we all need strength. It would be very strategic if we could prepare for adversity in the good times. You should also be firm in your conviction about being a servant of the Lord. David understood that his help could only come from God. Can you really build any lasting trust in anyone besides God? The family of God should certainly be a safe haven, but don't ever take your expectation away from God. David even knew he wasn't the first servant of God in his family tree. God has made some promises to your ancestors that you happen to benefit from. God has a specific will for your life, and yet it often stems from the prayers of your lineage.

REFLECTION:

January 28

"And Elisha prayed and said, 'O Lord, I pray, open his eyes that he may see.' And the LORD opened the servant's eyes and he saw; and behold, the mountain was full of horses and chariots of fire all around Elisha'" (II Kings 6:17 New American Standard).

Elisha was the prophet who wanted a double portion of his mentor Elijah's anointing. Can you see who is surrounding you? David mentioned being compassed about by his enemies on regular occasions. When danger is near, protection is nearer Sometimes you feel as though your enemies are closer than your allies. Prayer permits you to see what is invisible to your eyes.

Elisha knew that God wasn't about to abandon him in his greatest hour of need. There was another occasion where an angel sent from God slew 185,000 soldiers by himself! In this battle, the heavenly host actually outnumbered the earthly army. This had to be very encouraging to Elisha's young servant. There are many impressionable seekers watching to see how you handle perceived adversity. They need to know that your victories don't depend on your strength, wisdom, or expertise. You should certainly have all those advantages, but victory still rests with the Lord. The enemies were surrounding the city thinking they had the ultimate battle plan. Position yourself where you can see what God is doing. Pray for Him to encourage your comrades concerning His plan. Show up for the battle. Then, stand still and see the salvation of God.

REFLECTION:

January 29

"Rise up, O Lord, confront them, bring them down; rescue me from the wicked by your sword" (Psalms 17:13 New International Version).

This is David's plea for the Lord's involvement from his perspective. I marvel at how often we think God isn't involved. God is ALWAYS involved. He is either actively involved to be noticed or passively involved to be trusted. God's "rising" up takes on many vantage points. Are we still supposed to pray that God vanquish our opposition? I think we should examine God's participation and decide if He is really working on them or us! There are many times when God turns us over to the will of our adversaries to rid us of some destructive tendency. It's very hard to admit we might be the reason for our own downfall!

At least I will give David credit for not asking to be lifted. He asked that his enemies be brought low. The sword of the Lord is His word. The word of God has tremendous profit and should certainly be respected for the benefit it carries. The Bible's definition of a wicked person has more to do with their character than their actions. David's prayer requested that God go toe-to-toe with his enemies. A divine rescue normally includes more than we think it should. We must be subject to direction as well as being serious about deliverance.

REFLECTION:

January 30

"You understand, O Lord; remember me and care for me. Avenge me on my persecutors. You are long-suffering—do not take me away; think of how I suffer reproach for your sake" (Jeremiah 15:15 New International Version).

Isn't it comforting to know that God finds a myriad of ways to be so personal? He understands everything you face on a daily basis. He remembers His holy covenant He established with you. His "care package" includes benefits that are manifested in healing, strength, answered prayer, and spiritual prosperity among other things. Then, He even sweetens the relationship by coming to your rescue when your persecutors assume to take liberties with you. You must remember God is long-suffering with your enemies in the same manner He is with you. Don't think He has forgotten simply because vindication comes slowly. God will not disregard the things you endure for His sake. You can't be a prophet of God without knowing Him intimately. He will reveal Himself to you according to what He has designed for you to accomplish. You must take every opportunity to get to know Him better. Don't just get more information. Get more acquainted with His voice and the way He answers your call. God will never confine Himself to a reaction. He always responds according to His plan. Your path was engineered before the world appeared.

REFLECTION:

January 31

"Then Jesus said, 'I came into this world for judgment-as a Separator, in order that there may be separation [between those who believe on Me and those who reject Me]-to make the sightless see, and that those who see may become blind'" (John 9:39 Amplified Bible).

This is the response of Jesus when the Pharisees were investigating the recovery of sight to the man born blind. After numerous inquiries, the man was thrown out of the synagogue. Jesus found him and asked if he believed on the Son of Man. After his confession of faith, he worshipped Jesus. So, the Pharisees continued in their blindness, and believers gained spiritual eyesight. It's funny how Jesus didn't ask him about his faith until after it had cost him everything. His parents didn't want to stand up for him. He was already an outcast because of his blindness, and he had no one but himself. Jesus will wait to see just how bad you want Him. Sometimes the miracle you get from Him just gets you in more trouble. When all you have is yourself, He still wants you to deny yourself and worship Him. Human nature wants to lean or depend on something or someone else. God will remove all of your crutches, traditions, common sense, rationale, logic, emotion, heritage, lineage, ambition, security, confidence, and any other created thing—requiring only faith. The irony is that we tend to depend on what we get from Him more than we depend on Him!

REFLECTION:

FEBRUARY

February 1

"And Moses said unto the people, 'Fear ye not, standstill, and see the salvation of the Lord, which he will show to you today: for the Egyptians whom ye have seen today, ye shall see them again no more forever'" (Exodus 14:13 King James Version).

There are many things that could be going through your mind as you are on your way to the promise. The Israelites were just talking about how they should have stayed in Egypt. When things get tight, you normally second guess yourself. Did I really do the right thing? Is God still waiting for me at the end of THIS road? Just like you can't talk and listen, you can't walk and watch. The first thing God had to deal with was their fear. The fear of man shouldn't negate the reverence of God. Secondly, stand still and see means you should "watch" while God "does." Since you're not afraid anymore, you can see. If you were afraid, your eyes would have probably been shut. You are standing in anticipation, not standing paralyzed.

The salvation of the Lord happens constantly and consistently on a daily basis. God deals with your adversaries while you sleep, while you work, while you serve, while you worship, while you pray, and certainly while you witness. There is a day coming when God will deal with the opposition PERMANENTLY! The Egyptians used the people of God for personal gain. God knows who is for you and who is against you. Stand firm in your declaration. Keep your feet firmly entrenched in the truth of God's word. Relax, God's in charge.

REFLECTION:

February 2

"But I discipline my body and make it my slave, so that, after I have preached to others, I myself will not be disqualified" (I Corinthians 9:27 New American Standard).

Paul understood the importance of practicing what he preached. There are too many people who espouse the saying, "Do as I say and not as I do." That position cannot be supported anywhere in scripture. Various portions of the Bible tell us that we should be examples. Paul knew he was called to live in relationship first, then labor to form disciples. To be disqualified doesn't mean a loss of salvation, but rather a "setting aside" whenever God wants a vessel. Your flesh is constantly working in opposition to the will of God. As you can see, it is possible to keep your will under subjection. The ultimate hypocrite is one who justifies his own actions while condemning everyone else. Notice how Paul said he disciplines HIMSELF! We actually have power over no one but ourselves. The first part of this chapter is an expose on Paul's rights of Apostleship. The last part of the chapter is Paul's realization of his humanity. Whenever God calls you to preach, he has automatically called you to persevere.

REFLECTION:

February 3

"The Lord has rewarded me according to my righteousness, according to the cleanness of my hands in his sight" (Psalms 18:24 New International Version).

I know many of you are really struggling with this statement. Is this the same David who conspired to have another man's wife? Is this the same David who refused to discipline his own son Absalom? Is this the same David who numbered the children of Israel after being given explicit instructions not to? Yes, this is the same man! The things we remember David for have nothing to do with his righteousness. The righteousness of David isn't self-righteousness; it is God's righteousness. When God rewards you, He does it according to how you respond to the knowledge of Him. Yes, David committed grievous sin, but David also repented gloriously. Anyone can justify their actions behind their humanity. David knew that his hands were clean because God washed him. Do you REALLY know how God sees you? Let me give you a biblical example. When you read about the life of David in the book of Samuel, all of his human failures are mentioned. When you read about David in the book of Chronicles, none of his human failures are mentioned. God never excuses sin: He removes it! Behold the Lamb of God which takes away the sin of the world. You are forgiven if you want to be.

REFLECTION:

February 4

"Bear (endure, carry) one another's burdens and troublesome moral faults, and in this way fulfill and observe perfectly the law of Christ (the Messiah) and complete what is lacking [in your obedience to it]" (Galatians 6:2 Amplified Bible).

I had a recent conversation with a saint I value very much. As we were talking, the conversation turned to "needs." It occurred to me that Christians are fantastic at encouraging each other, yet seldom willing to meet each other's needs in a practical manner. Verse one in this chapter tells us to restore the overtaken. This verse tells us how. We must be willing to "spend" what we have. Bearing a burden means shouldering the load with the other person and making it bearable! What needs has God exposed to you? I'm not specifically talking about money. Although, money is included in what God gives you to use. The gifts you have should lighten the load of others. The godly and winsome elements of your personality should help others carry their load. We have the same obstacles as individuals that we have as congregations. We want others to come in and get it when Jesus said we should go out and give it. God demands we use what He has given us.

When you "help" another child of God, you receive help too. The only thing lacking in your faith is WORK! You would never hold back in trying to meet your own needs, so please don't do it to others. If you're afraid someone will take advantage of you, here's what you should do. Ask God who needs what you have and how you should approach them. Sometimes He might have you do it anonymously. You won't be victimized if you're making the decision instead of responding to a request. Do your best to get His best!

REFLECTION:

_____

_____

_____

41

February 5

"What is man, that he could be pure, Or he who is born of a woman, that he should be righteous?" (Job 15:14 New American Standard).

Job's friends didn't really help him much, but they did the best they could with the information provided to them. They insisted that Job had to offend God to be facing the type of calamity he faced. Job was a man of integrity, but his condition made it difficult to understand how a man of integrity should have to endure such pain. Job continued to proclaim his innocence despite his outward appearance.

Do people look at you and assume they know how God feels about you? Of course they do! The Bible is clear that no one is righteous, so God has to give us His righteousness. Job didn't actually "do" anything that deserved the satanic onslaught he endured. However, you don't have to "do" anything to be hated by the devil. All of us were born in sin, so from one perspective we all deserve whatever bad things happen. Only the grace of God prevents bad things from happening. Even after you come to Christ, you still commit sins on a regular basis. God must forgive us in order to make it possible for us to fellowship with Him. When God responds at the end of this book, He straightens out Job and his friends. Because Job was still God's man, He corrected Job so he could pray for his friends. You are in no position to pray for your friends until God corrects you first. If you're in the middle of a situation you don't deserve, don't bother proclaiming your innocence. Plead for God's mercy!

REFLECTION:

February 6

"He is your praise; he is your God, who performed for you those great and awesome wonders you saw with your own eyes" (Deuteronomy 10:21 New International Version).

The book of Deuteronomy is the second opportunity for Moses to discuss and promote the Law of God. Moses wants the people of God to whole-heartedly follow God. He reiterates the blessings of adherence and reminds them of the punishment associated with disobedience. Even today, God has done many things in your life that deserves praise. Just the fact that He is God makes Him deserving of worship. You were once in the bondage of sin and unable to please God, and He delivered you. As you began to pursue your liberty, the enemy began to close in on you. Then, God waited until just the right moment and eliminated him. He miraculously provides for you even though you exist far from home. There have been many things over the years that you could easily forget. Over the next few days, you should carefully examine what God has been up to in your life. He has a strategic plan that involves your friends, your education, your job, your church, your associations, your spouse, and your ambitions. Try to connect events in your past with what's happening now. Then, commit to praying about your future. Encourage yourself with scriptural declarations. God completes what He starts. See yourself as a work in progress headed for completion.

REFLECTION:

February 7

"Wait on the Lord, and keep his way, and he shall exalt thee to inherit the land: when the wicked are cut off, thou shalt see it" (Psalms 37:34 King James Version).

Proverbs tells us, "The way that seems right to us leads to death." It may not be a literal death, but a separation from God feels like a literal death. The important thing about navigating through life is discovering God's way. Most people interviewed would say God moves much too slowly. He seems to find the scenic route to the goal. He wants you to inherit the things He has in store for you.

An inheritance is never a quick alternative for temporary rescue. A real inheritance takes a lifetime to build so it can carry the heir through a lifetime of testing. The beauty is you didn't do any of the work for the inheritance you qualify for. The least you can do is wait for it. God just wants to be trusted. He is trying to put you in the most advantageous position possible. He will eliminate the wicked from "your" land without ruining the land. Your vantage point will be one of observation. When God moves, there won't be any doubt about who did it. If He always moved swiftly, you would begin to either take Him for granted or try to order Him around. Your attitudes about His decisions reflect whether you want Him in charge. God is fully expecting you to be in charge one day. Until that day comes, He is fully expecting you to let go.

REFLECTION:

February 8

"For [simply] consider your own call, brethren; not many [of you were considered to be] wise, according to human estimates and standards; not many influential and powerful; not many of high and noble birth" (I Corinthians 1:26 Amplified Bible).

Things really haven't changed much. The Jews are still seeking the "sign" while the Greeks are still seeking "wisdom." It seems like we crave more evidence even after we come to know God. Sometimes we go a little overboard in respect of the opinions of others. There must be some balanced approach to living the same simple gospel we preach. If the foolishness of God is wiser than men, why do we constantly consult the wisdom of men? The Spirit of God knows the mind of God. The Spirit of God also dwells in us. I constantly marvel at how God bypasses the obvious choices and inhabits the obscure. Verse 28 in this same chapter talks about God's pleasure in choosing the lowborn, insignificant, and branded by contempt. We could also say: forgotten, despised, overlooked, under qualified, inferior, handicapped, etc. We still look for people of reputation instead of asking and praying for people of influence. What if the best person to solve your problem never wrote it in a book? When God says, "Ask, seek, and knock," something tells me He wants us to ask, seek, and knock. He saved you so He could use you as an example to others. The chances are great that He has chosen other unknowns, so they can help you too. If your salvation came in the unlikely form of a humble servant, your solution probably has that same form.

REFLECTION:

February 9

"Anyone who failed to appear within three days would forfeit all his property, in accordance with the decision of the officials and elders and would himself be expelled from the assembly of the exiles" (Ezra 10:8 New International Version).

God was displeased about His people taking foreign wives, and Ezra knew it. The leaders decided they needed to hold a solemn assembly, confess, repent, and appeal to the mercy of God for restoration. People today won't even confess, let alone repent. Ezra knew the blessings of God were being stifled due to the rebellious state of the people. God has no problem correcting a nation the same way He corrects an individual. If you read this chapter, it lists the names of those who were guilty. God gives us tremendous grace by keeping our faults anonymous. I would love to see a coalition of local leadership call for a gathering of confession and repentance. It would be nothing to rent a convention center or an arena and compel people from all over this region to purge themselves. It bothers me that all we seem to be concerned with is how we can appear more successful. Ezra's generation was so serious that whoever didn't participate was removed from the fellowship and rendered penniless! God wants us to chasten ourselves, so He won't have to. We spend billions of dollars in building-centered ministry. Could we not spend rental fees for people-centered ministry? Maybe then we would have a REAL revival.

REFLECTION:

February 10

"Do not judge, and you will not be judged. Do not condemn, and you will not be condemned. Forgive, and you will be forgiven" (Luke 6:37 New International Version).

This verse is clear as it re ates to God's expectations. Many times, people will hide behind their own contexts and interpretations. Jesus clearly says we shouldn't judge, shouldn't condemn, and should forgive. To judge is to make a determination concerning the heart of another individual. How can we decide about a person's heart when God doesn't allow us to see it? We are to evaluate actions without determining motive. To condemn is to sentence someone without all the facts. Sometimes we condemn others based on our own bias or prejudice. 1 Corinthians tells us that love hopes all things and believes all things. We shouldn't be naïve, but we must always leave room for the possibility of change. Finally, to forgive means we have completely healed from harm, and it doesn't affect our objectivity. We won't argue the differences between forgiving and forgetting but consider this: God knows all things and says I will remember your sin no more. He means that even though He knows what you did, it won't affect His treatment of you, nor His actions toward you.

REFLECTION:

47

February 11

"Therefore, this is what the Sovereign Lord says, 'My servants will eat, but you will go hungry; my servants will drink, but you will go thirsty; my servants will rejoice, but you will be put to shame'" (Isaiah 65:13 New International Version).

This is what God says to those who forsake Him, to those who don't listen to Him, who spread a table for fortune, and who basically live as though they won't ever give account to Him. God often finds it necessary to encourage His people because they aren't always in encouraging circumstances. God makes it clear He will turn the tables in favor of His servants. Don't always assume He will wait until heaven to get even. There are things He does in your life currently that show His desire to help you. Many of these passages speak of a permanent state that God's people will rest in. Keep your faith intact since you know it's not in vain. I find comfort in the fact that this verse gives the "Sovereign" title to God. In other words, whatever may be happening right now doesn't change the ultimate victorious outcome. Everything in the universe will yield to God's desire. Remember how Jesus made a "triumphal entry into Jerusalem? That entry was made before He faced the cross! Everything that happens in your will contributes to taking you to your destiny. The enemy sometimes hitches a ride in your life, but God always stays behind the wheel.

REFLECTION:

February 12

"I will thank You and confide in you forever, because You have done it [delivered me and kept me safe]. I will wait, hope and expect in Your name, for it is good, in the presence of Your saints [You kind and pious ones]" (Psalms 52:9 Amplified Bible).

The things God HAS done should have set up your expectation concerning what He WILL do. Thanks, praise, confidence, patience, hope, and expectation should be the order of the day. If you're honest, you have worried about what God decided or will decide to do. God has both delivered (past tense) and kept you safe. Safety is only required when danger is present.

Sometimes I think we see life as safe, and once in a while danger comes. If you're a Christian, danger is always present. God is constantly working to keep you protected. The way we express our reliance on God is beneficial for even the saints. We can avoid lots of physical issues when the spiritual perspective is healthy. Most of our problems result from a lack of trust in the word of God. It sounds simple, but it is a profound truth. The Lord has a very impressive resume even if He felt like retiring right now. Thousands of years hold the answers to all of life's questions. Faith includes "substance" and "evidence." So many people need a LIFT. The psalms' treasure house is waiting for you to simply find a word of encouragement.

REFLECTION:

February 13

"Your way [in delivering Your people] was through the sea, and Your paths through the great waters; yet Your footsteps were not traceable but were obliterated" (Psalms 77:19 Amplified Bible).

As you walk with God, you never know what to expect. Since God is the ruler of everything, He can use people, nature, angels, and even demons to accomplish His will. Don't ever be dismayed concerning His choice of vessel. I love the fact that God doesn't allow Himself to be put in any receptacle. Water always washes away footprints. The footprints of God are not traceable. His voice can't be recorded, and His ways are past finding out. Your journey with Him will always be completely by faith. He will give you good ideas and modify them as you implement them. He will give you vision and amend your agenda. He will speak to you intimately. Then, He will impose His will. He will compel you to go, and steer you as you go. He will whisper success to you and turn the hearts of authorities to favor you.

God doesn't want you to "expect" anything from Him, except that He will show up. Your deliverance will take on many forms, but no matter what, it will always be deliverance! The sea was a daunting foe to those who sailed. It is impossible to know how the sea will react, and it is impossible to know how God will provide. Don't panic because Jesus is asleep on the boat; just be thankful that He is always on board!

REFLECTION:

February 14

"The meek also shall increase their joy in the Lord, and the poor among men shall rejoice and exult in the Holy One of Israel" (Isaiah 29:19 Amplified Bible).

Bad circumstances decrease the hopes of the afflicted. There are many who think their situation will never change. Their experience has normally been: "two steps forward and three steps back." If the people of God live out the mandates given, poverty wouldn't be a world-wide epidemic. Thank God for those who have a heart for the under-served because God does. The promises He declares are meant to restore hope to the hopeless. He wants all of us to know that our future is much better than our past. What else can cause the poor to rejoice? Jesus said that the poor have the gospel preached to them. This may not sound like a big deal, but God placed His entire fortune in the hope of His Son. The gospel is the good news that things WILL get better. Your days WILL get brighter; your God WILL get even; your enemies WILL be defeated. I want God to be the national hope of America the same way He was the national hope of Israel. Increasing joy is the result of building on your relationship with God. Times may be hard, but God isn't subject to the times. God never finishes last; He never even finishes second.

REFLECTION:

February 15

"Behold, I am going to deal at that time with all your oppressors, I will save the lame, and gather the outcast, and I will turn their shame into praise and renown in all the earth" (Zephaniah 3:19 New American Standard).

Although Zephaniah is a short prophetic writing, it is full of the fury of God's wrath. This book teaches us a great lesson about the love of God. Even though judgment is necessary, God never lets the story end on that somber note. God promises His people that He will restore their dignity, their reputation, and their supremacy over their enemies.

God has the power to change ownership. He can cause the rich to be poor, and the poor to become rich. One very important ingredient that you add to His mixture is PRAISE! God deserves praise, and He delights in praise. It is a tremendous honor to be appointed for praise. The people of God should know it isn't about how strong you are at the beginning of the race (or even in the middle of the race), but how strong you finish. God is a finisher! God encourages finishers. The earth is the Lord's, and all of its fullness. The world and all of its inhabitants belong to Him. Even when His anger causes chastening to be released on His people, He will still remember mercy.

REFLECTION:

February 16

"For I am about to do a brand-new thing. See, I have already begun! Do you not see it? I will make a pathway through the wilderness for my people to come home. I will create rivers for them in the desert" (Isaiah 43:19 New Living Translation).

Here we are again at the beginning of a new year. I really appreciate the way God gives us fresh starts all throughout life. I pray for each of you reading this that God will give you new insights, new vision, new inspiration, new creativity, new hope, renewed faith, and new perspective. Since you can't put new wine into old wineskins, I pray also that He will rejuvenate YOU! What is a pathway through the wilderness? I believe it means God will give you life in dead places. God will quicken your dead relationships, and He will also use you to be the breath of anointed fresh air in stagnate circles of "so-called" fellowship. Aren't you tired of leaving Christian gatherings under whelmed? When God does something, He wants it to be memorable. When He bothers to get involved in anything, it should have the breath of life. Your life is leading you home. A river in a dry place doesn't need interpreting. If He can feed you in front of your enemies, why can't He give you drink in a dry place? Don't you see Him at work already? Since He is already pouring and outpouring, why would you continue in your thirst? Drink now! I declare again that this year will be the best year you ever had! May your new year stimulate newness in you. HAPPY NEW YOU!

REFLECTION:

February 17

"But I say, don't resist an evil person! If you are slapped on the right cheek, turn the other, too" (Matthew 5:39 New Living Translation).

The next time you're feeling good about your level of Christian commitment, read the Sermon on the Mount in chapters 5, 6, and 7 of Matthew. It is also affectionately called the Olivet discourse. If you have a red-letter Bible, please notice that these chapters are entirely RED with the exception of the first verse in chapter five and the last verse in chapter seven, which serve as introduction and conclusion. Follow this rule: whatever is RED in my Bible <u>must</u> be READ from my Bible! Jesus is taking this opportunity to make sure we have a clear understanding of God's intentions. God has extremely high standards that we can't reach in our own strength. As a matter of fact, God's standards are perfect, and we aren't. Turn the other cheek when slapped? I don't think so! Well, God thinks so and says so. Does that mean we have to be a human kickball? Does that make us wimpy pushovers? The answer is "NO" to both questions. God wants us to make a priority of overcoming evil with good. The wrath of man doesn't produce the righteousness of God. There is a plan in place for your enemies, and you need to follow that plan. It is more important to God that your light shines brighter than your defense mechanisms.

REFLECTION:

February 18

"Blessed are the pure in heart: for they shall see God" (Matthew 5:8 King James Version).

This verse doesn't have a lot of words, but it does have a lot of meaning. To be pure in your heart shows you have a relationship with God that transcends time and outlasts circumstances. Your heart holds the hopes you have, the dreams you embrace, and the expectation of something wholesome. What does it mean to "see" God? I believe it means you will experience His special favor against all opposition. I believe it means you will have peace that boggles the minds of your antagonists. I believe it means God will shine through everything else that happens in your life. I believe it means you will know full joy from always giving Him the benefit of the doubt. And when you see God, others can't help but see His reflection in you. This is so much more than the power of positive thinking. Positive thinking never reaches the point of changing your environment, so it always focuses on your perspective. God promises your faith is the reason for your perspective and because of that, He will transform everything else. God's image is so strong; He causes everything else to change.

REFLECTION:

February 19

"Therefore, dear friends, since you already know this, be on your guard so that you may not be carried away by the error of lawless men and fall from your secure position" (II Peter 3:17 New International Version).

Peter is exhorting the people of God to know what the word of God says. He even mentions the messages of Paul as a reference to know what God is up to. We must guard the word of God in our hearts. There are many convincing arguments that compete for our endorsement. Your position is secure as long as you know it really isn't yours. The position you adhere to is Christ's. The wisdom and beauty of the enemy is very persuasive, so look for God to expose him. There is a lot of truth in the lie of the enemy, yet God still wants you to be aware of his devices. You must know the difference between liberty and lawlessness. God gives you great liberty, although you are always under His authority. Don't come up with your own ideas. Your position in Christ is based on His plan for you. Peter is an authority on the thin line between denial and betrayal. Error is typically based on those who feel they have a corner on the market of revelation. A fall is an unplanned descent from a place of safety.

Peter knew what it meant to be restored and be a voice of reason. Take a close look at the things you think you know, so you can make sound decisions concerning your destiny. Don't be vague about your beliefs, and God won't be vague about His peace.

REFLECTION:

February 20

"Therefore I, a prisoner for serving the Lord, beg you to lead a life worthy of your calling, for you have been called by God" (Ephesians 4:1 New Living Translation).

Congratulations, you have been chosen to do a job by the CEO of the universe. Before you start calling all of your friends to brag about this wonderful position, there are a few things you should understand. You are required to bless them who curse you, turn the other cheek when slapped, give them your shirt when they take your coat, love your enemies, pray for the ones you know are malicious towards you, and give your adversaries food and drink. Now: go ahead and brag to your friends.

Sometimes the things God asks us to do seem impossible! Paul served the Lord faithfully and it got him landed in prison. Do you ever feel as though you've been imprisoned for serving the Lord? God still used Paul while he was locked away or death row. The prison letters in the bible have been used to bless countless millions. I believe God wants you to enjoy your life here and certainly in the hereafter. But I must confess that sometimes I feel as though He wants us to loathe this existence and yearn for His literal, physical presence. I admire Paul's attitude because I don't think I would have responded the same way. Do whatever God has called you to do without whining and excuses. He knows you're not qualified to work for Him. You will be much better off when YOU realize you're not qualified.

REFLECTION:

February 21

"And there are also many other things which Jesus did, which if they were written in detail, I suppose that even the world itself would not contain the books which were written" (John 21:25 New American Standard).

The gospel writers listed many things concerning the life of Christ. The books written by John really show the miraculous influence of Jesus. Have you ever been so impacted by someone that you wanted everyone else to know them? John believed that he and everyone else could write about Jesus, and the earth wouldn't be a large enough library for the volumes. Each of us should do our own writing about the difference God makes in our lives.

The Bible was left on record for us to read and be convinced that Jesus came to save those who were lost. These writings are a form of "testimony." Your writings may not get published or get widespread publicity, but someone could still be convinced that Jesus is REAL! His disciples weren't just trying to sell books; they were trying to change lives. If one of the unwritten things Jesus did involved you, consider the possibility that your journal may be pulled out of a box 100 years from now and lead someone to Christ. God performs miracles through very mysterious means. Faith comes in a variety of forms, but it always makes a difference. If you don't have the boldness to speak the word, consider writing it and leaving it to inspire someone else.

REFLECTION:

February 22

"Render to all what is due them: tax to whom tax is due, custom to whom custom; fear to whom fear; honor to whom honor" (Romans 13:7 New American Standard).

I find it quite interesting that we are only usually concerned about what someone is due when they are over us in authority. Well, the people under us in authority might be due something too. There's just something about the human heart that wants to be the greatest. Even disciples wondered about this and jockeyed for chief kingdom seats. I see nothing here that says anyone has to "earn" their respect. It would be good if people did earn respect, but God says to GIVE them their due. God has ordained power and authority. He even tells servants to submit to unreasonable overseers. This verse also mentions customs. Another version translated it as import taxes.

How many times have you "forgotten" to tell the border agent about the stuff in your trunk purchased in Canada? This probably seems like splitting hairs to you, so won't continue. I think it is good Christian ethics to see yourself as the servant in every situation. You don't have to yield your authority; just use it wisely because you too are under authority. Paul gave instructions knowing that he was under Roman rule. He didn't agree with their tyranny, but he did understand that God is ultimately in charge of his life. Sometimes I think we expect to live to be at least 100 years old with good health, good fortune, good friends, and good times at all times. If life was like that, who would be waiting for Heaven?

REFLECTION:

59

February 23

"If you are wise and understand God's ways, live a life of steady goodness so that only good deeds will pour forth. And if you don't brag about the good you do, then you will be truly wise" (James 3:13 New Living Translation).

This verse really doesn't need commentary. Jesus said that He always did what pleased His Father. Today's version of Christianity has very little if any personal conviction. If you want to know where you stand, you must ask yourself two fundamental questions. First: what does my relationship with God keep me from doing, even though I like it? Second: what does my relationship with God compel me to do, even though I don't like it?

Jesus had power because He surrendered His will. Many Christians today are trying to discover how to be like Jesus without doing what He did. Let me know how that turns out. The good deeds that pour out of your life only happen because you're in God's hands, the same way a glass pours out its contents when the holder tips it. Wisdom is knowing, understanding, and applying God's ways. You are only a vessel, but to be only a vessel in the Master's hands is a rare privilege. Blessings have become so common that people rarely watch their conduct. The book of James talks more about wisdom than we give it credit for. Although it is a very short book, there is still plenty of substance to it. Humility is the perfect balance between your performance and God's control. I think the verse is really trying to teach us how to let your life speak of your wisdom more than your lips.

REFLECTION:

February 24

"You have not strengthened the weak or healed the sick or bound up the injured. You have not brought back the strays or searched for the lost. You have ruled them harshly and brutally" (Ezekiel 34:4 New International Version).

Ezekiel was chosen to be a voice of chastisement for the kinds of leaders that are characterized by selfishness. God wants His people to be cared for with His sensitivity. He has chosen many to represent His compassion and gentleness. God still expects His leaders to be firm, but that doesn't negate His desire to restore. Leaders can't assume that everyone struggles because of rebellion. Some people are under severe attack and really want to please God. If someone is weak, sick, injured, stray, or lost; the emphasis should be on restoration. God's job is to deal with the hard-hearted; our job is to represent God.

How many people treat others the way God treats them? God promised to be a personal shepherd to His people. He has fulfilled that promise to you in the person of Christ. The emphasis today has shifted to personal gain, personal satisfaction, and portraying a form of godliness. God doesn't grant you success to make people admire you; He grants you success so people can admire Him! The brutality in the body of Christ tells us how far we have fallen short of the mandate. It is extremely brutal to give poison and expect health. God wants you to be healthy, so if you're not, trust Him to lead you to fresh water.

REFLECTION:

February 25

"See what [an incredible] quality of love the Father has given (shown, bestowed on) us, that we should [be permitted to] be named and called and counted the children of God! And so we are! The reason that the world does not know (recognize, acknowledge) us, is that it does not know (recognize, acknowledge) Him" (I John 3:1 Amplified Bible).

Pull over from your hectic break-neck world and take the time to digest what God has given you. We often spend far too much time chasing what we don't have and devaluing what we do have. God has manifested His love toward us in incredible ways so we can confidently move through life. There isn't a moment where He stops declaring His love for you. It's one thing to have feelings and another thing entirely to declare those feelings by what you do. You are a child of God. Is there any higher privilege? Is there any greater heritage? Can you receive a more noble inheritance? Don't be dismayed because the world rejects you. The world is supposed to be estranged to its foreigners. You are a citizen of another country. Expect to receive similar treatment to Christ's. He still intends to bless you in front of your enemies. He took the pain out of your gain. Quality defines what you get from God because infinity defines Who it comes from. Actually, infinity is still inadequate to define who it comes from.

REFLECTION:

February 26

"For since He Himself was tempted in that which He has suffered, He is able to come to the aid of those who are tempted" (Hebrews 2:18 New American Standard).

On many occasions in life, you face situations that make you think nobody really understands. You feel as though no one has walked in your shoes; no one knows how you feel. There is nothing new under the sun, not even your circumstances or feelings. It should give you great consolation to know that there are footsteps in front of you. Jesus has already been where you're going. Jesus has already felt what you're feeling.

Sometimes praise doesn't even make sense to you. Worship must become part of your essence while praise becomes a "natural" function. The Bible tells us that we live, move, and have our being in Him. Do you think you can survive just making Him a part of your day? Can you withstand the onslaught of your enemy with Jesus as an afterthought? He assumed your nature so He could "relate" to anything you encounter. When you seek the aid of someone, it brings a measure of relief when you don't have to explain yourself. Jesus will come to your aid because you need Him, not just because you ask Him. God is well acquainted with deliverance methods. All of His procedures work extremely well.

REFLECTION:

February 27

"I urge you, brothers, to watch out for those who cause divisions and put obstacles in your way that are contrary to the teaching you have learned. Keep away from them" (Romans 16:17 New International Version).

Paul knows that your convictions and teachings don't make you invulnerable. When you keep company with those who are different than you, either they will start acting like you, or more likely, you will start acting like them. Unbelievers always make your path difficult, no matter how nice or funny they are. How can two walk together unless they agree? That doesn't mean you have to be exactly alike in every respect; you just need to have the same faith.

Sometimes Christians cause divisions too. You are never strong enough to rest on your own laurels. An obstacle is usually an unexpected detour from the road you expected to travel. When Paul says to watch out for those, I believe he means protecting yourself from their persuasive arguments. You would be surprised how convincing a lie can sound if you listen to it long enough. Lies have a way of mingling with your logic and rationale until it becomes a reasonable alternative. These reasonable alternatives are called strongholds. The things you have learned are based on the truth of scripture. Anything else besides what you have learned is based on doctrinal seduction. God requires participation from each of us in our own salvation. We are required to make sound decisions that aren't always based on creature comforts.

REFLECTION:

February 28

"But you, O God, do see trouble and grief; you consider it to take it in hand. The victim commits himself to you; you are the helper of the fatherless" (Psalms 10:14 New International Version).

The people that don't know God live as though He doesn't exist. They breathe His air, drink His water, eat His food, and refuse to acknowledge Him. God still sees everything and governs everything. Trouble rises when you encounter things that are greater than you and lose perspective. Grief overtakes you when you experience a great sense of loss, and you struggle to press forward.

God considers your problems and takes them upon Himself. In other words, your problems are His problems. Are you a victim? If so, God is waiting for you to rely on Him instead of taking matters into your own hands. Victims don't always know who the villains are. God knows perfectly well who exploited you. Getting even isn't as important as getting into the presence of God. In biblical times, the father was practically irreplaceable in the family structure. He was the protector, provider, and priest of the home. God promises to be the helper of those who lack the covering security of a father. The psalmist shows us how to see God as He really is. Life will place you face to face with trials that test your faith. You must answer every challenge with a determination to see God in everything. If you don't see Him yet, look closer. Believe me, He's there.

REFLECTION:

MARCH

March 1

"One hand full of rest is better than two fists full of labor and striving after wind" (Ecclesiastes 4:6 New American Standard).

Solomon takes the opportunity to tell us about the contrasts he has encountered in his life. It is much better to have one hand full in the will of God than two hands full outside of God's will. Rest is what you can look forward to after having done work. When God created the world, He labored for six days and then rested for one day. We sometimes act as though rest comes before work when God makes it clear that work comes before rest. Striving after the wind is equivalent to trying to predict how God is going to move.

As people of God, we need to be open to however God decides to move as opposed to trying to predict His movements. God can accomplish His will in completely unorthodox methods. We have the option of deciding how we will allow God to move in our lives. Do you know what rest really is? Rest is what Jesus gives you in contrast to what you give Him. You give Him labor and heavy burdens, and He gives you rest. Striving for things gives the picture of clawing, scratching, and pushing for things to happen. Solomon knows that it is best to confess your weaknesses to God in order for Him to perfect the things lacking in you. Examine your life to see where you have not functioned in the center of God's will. The sooner God can get your attention, the sooner you can strategically position yourself for the next move. God just might want to do something with you that He hasn't done with anyone else.

Reflection:

March 2

"We have this hope as an anchor for the soul, firm and secure. It enters the inner sanctuary behind the curtain" (Hebrews 6:19 New International Version).

Is your hope in God? The Bible also says that "hope that is seen is not hope." Faith is your vessel while hope is the anchor that keeps your vessel from drifting. It is typically the invisible object that works the hardest. The anchor isn't visible while it's stabilizing the vessel. The roots of a plant aren't visible, yet they support what is visible. This verse is tremendous because it teaches us a principle concerning the "sound" of hope.

The High Priest wasn't seen when he went behind the veil. The hope of the people was steadfast as long as they "heard" the bell tied to his garment. Faith comes by "hearing." Every promise of God was a "spoken" promise. The worst thing that could ever happen to a believer would be for God to be SILENT. He that has an ear, let him "hear" what the Spirit says to the church. The disciples in the upper room heard the "sound" of a rushing mighty wind. Today's believers are waiting for the "sound" of the trumpet, which indicates our rescue, and prepares us for the coming battle. Because God cannot lie, we have a full assurance of His ability and willingness to deliver 100% on EVERY promise. Your feelings will deceive you; your thoughts will mislead you; your friends will forsake you. Your enemies will pursue you, but your God will sustain you.

REFLECTION:

March 3

"For I tell you that many prophets and kings wanted to see what you see but did not see it, and hear what you hear but did not hear it" (Luke 10:24 New International Version).

When was the last time you stopped to think just how incredibly blessed you REALLY are? You are living in awesome days. I know the times are perilous, but the days are precious. In biblical terms, the word "precious" meant *rare*. Jesus was telling His disciples how privileged they were to see the Man of faith that others wished they could see. You too have the internal witness of the Spirit of God. Prophets and kings were the chosen leaders of God for his people and other nations. We have it better than the best. We have the testimony of God the Father, the sacrifice of God the Son, and the seal of God the Holy Spirit.

You are in a very select minority. The work of the Spirit in the Old Testament provided an expectation in God's people while His work in the New Testament provided an earnest. He is the down payment that proves God's full intent to pay the balance. The balance won't be satisfied until you receive your new body. The point is: God has done a marvelous work in your life IF you have a relationship with Him. If not, everything in your life is utterly meaningless in the scope of eternity. Give in to the "pull" on your life, so you can see and hear things that countless others couldn't.

REFLECTION:

March 4

"He who has knowledge spares his words, and a man of understanding has a cool spirit" (Proverbs 17:27 Amplified Bible).

This principle doesn't exactly hold true in American halls of justice where fast talking and quick thinking make others think you know what you're doing. God isn't impressed by who can talk the most or the fastest. When it comes to the things of God, quality supersedes quantity. The sparing of words drastically reduces thoughtless injury. How many times have you wished you could just "take it back?" It would seem logical that a person's knowledge would be evident by what they have to say. Sometimes you can be brilliant by knowing what not to say.

What does it mean to have a cool spirit? It's not some modern context of being well-liked. A cool spirit is to be even tempered. One who doesn't panic yet knows when to be expeditious. Solomon knew that it is fitting to consider what you say, and then say it with balance and discretion. When we find ourselves in deep circumstances, it is typically our use of words that can sink us deeper or get us out. Take your time and form thoughts, before you form words, before you form actions. Words carry the power of life and death. Understanding will allow you to accurately assess a situation, commit it to prayer, and determine the best course of action for your involvement.

REFLECTION:

March 5

"He who was seated on the throne said, 'I am making everything new!' Then he said, 'Write this down, for these words are trustworthy and true'" (Revelation 21:5 New International Version).

To be seated on a throne shows power, authority, influence, and supremacy. God is sovereign, and the throne He is seated on only fits Him! Chapter 21 comes after chapter 20 where all of God's enemies were permanently vanquished. He has no formidable foes; He only tolerates the course of evil in order to give us a choice because He poured out His wrath on Jesus. He made things new because it was time for His new creations to enjoy a new environment, an environment not subject to the former challenges and not susceptible to any evil influences.

God wanted this written because He is a God of His word. The Lord wanted to leave this on record for those who would need renewed hope in order to endure. God certainly is trustworthy and true. The book of Revelation shows each of God's people how the story really ends. Even death can't defeat the purposes of God. No matter how bad your life ends in time; it begins on a good note in eternity. So, actually the book of Revelation is about your glorified beginning, which has no end. Jesus died to restore our image to God, and once you have that image, there can be no altering of it EVER again.

REFLECTION:

March 6

"Everything has already been decided. It was known long ago what each person would be. So, there's no use arguing with God about your destiny" (Ecclesiastes 6:10 New Living Translational).

I find this verse particularly intriguing because it gives a compelling argument. Does this mean that it doesn't matter what you do? Did Solomon possibly believe that his actions were already determined? I don't want to expound on this verse. I simply want to give you things to consider. You will have many different "moods" and perspectives as you live through the things God has put in your path. Sometimes you will see yourself as a robot that can't change an outcome. Sometimes you will feel determined to make a difference. Sometimes you will get tired of feeling. Sometimes you will feel particularly vulnerable. Sometimes you will feel invincible. The way you see this verse will change according to your moods, but the meaning of this verse never changes.

I love the way God allowed Solomon to express himself and still permitted it to be scripture. All scripture is inspired by God, including this one. God does know what will be. He knows what is, and He knows what was. The human problem is that we think we know more than we actually know. God stimulates each of us to learn about Him. How can you learn about Him if you're constantly examining anything else? I believe I read something that said, "Depression looks down. Worry looks around. Hope looks up." I may not have gotten it exactly right, but you get my point.

REFLECTION:

_____

_____

_____

_____

_____

_____

March 7

"So, the law was put in charge to lead us to Christ that we might be justified by faith" (Galatians 3:24 New International Version).

Many today choose to soothe their consciences by the virtues of religion and the values of tradition. God is the foundation of "religion" and the "ignition" for traditions. Amazingly, He has been left out of many religions and traditions. The law of God was given, so we would realize that works alone cannot please God. The law could only be kept by someone perfect. God's commands include accountability for your thoughts. I don't know ANYONE who can claim mastery over the things they think about. God does promise us that when we commit our works to Him, our thoughts will be established. I believe that means He will bring to pass what we want to do because we work to glorify Him.

Everything God did after the fall was done to point us to our need for divine help. Since we need a "helper" like the Holy Spirit even after conversion, why would you think you could please God in your own strength? God gave strength and authority to the law, so He could make the law submit to the strength and authority of Jesus. Jesus fulfilled the law by knowing how much He needed a close connection with the Father. You fulfill the law by a faith relationship with Him because He kept the law.

REFLECTION:

_____

_____

_____

_____

_____

_____

_____

_____

March 8

"I know, O Lord, that a man's life is not his own; it is not for man to direct his steps" (Jeremiah 10:23 New International Version).

You would be surprised to discover how many people consider themselves masters of their own destiny. No matter how hard you try, nothing would be achieved or attained without the mercy of God. Even though we live in a land of "opportunity," even though you make your own decisions, even though you were fortunate enough to be well educated, and even though you are extremely talented, everything you have comes from someone, not somewhere.

Jeremiah learned what it meant to be a spokesperson for God. If you're going to speak for the Lord, get ready to keep pen and paper handy because you will ALWAYS be learning. The foolishness of God is wiser than men, so don't consider yourself wise in the things of God. You are clay in the hands of an all-wise God. Your steps are ordered by the Lord. How can you direct your own life? You don't control what happens to you or in you. Your destiny is the result of a plan that makes room for your decisions. God shows grace, mercy, compassion, kindness, favor, and good-will to whomever He sees fit. Be thankful He isn't simply giving you what He owes you.

REFLECTION:

March 9

"The Lord nurses them when they are sick and eases their pain and discomfort" (Psalms 41:3 New Living Translation).

This is a promise of the Lord to those who are considerate and gracious to the poor. The Bible tells us that the poor will always exist among us. I believe God wants to see how we respond to the less fortunate. He constantly mentions how He feels about the widows, the fatherless, and the destitute. When you show kindness to others, God is careful not to forget you. I believe He even shows mercy to those who don't know Him and are kind to the poor. The Bible mentions how people will be separated on judgment day. Some will be rewarded because Jesus said they ministered to Him when He was naked, and a stranger, sick, imprisoned, and hungry.

You never know how far a kind gesture will travel. You could be the very one that allows a person's hope to continue beyond today. Suicidal thoughts run rampant when a person just can't get a break. Everyone has a breaking point, and I believe God wants us to help. He will be your caregiver when you give His kind of care. He will ease your pain and discomfort as you strive to represent Him in this heartless world. The Bible also says, "When you give to the poor and needy, you lend to the Lord." Pain and discomfort come in physical forms, mental forms, financial stress, and more. God wants others to find the same comforting relief in Him that you have found.

REFLECTION:

March 10

"It is good that he waits silently for the salvation of the LORD" (Lamentations 3:26 New American Standard).

Although this verse is short, it still provides a multitude of insight for those sitting in expectation of God's move. Many of God's people spend lots of time concerned about what God will do for them. The truth is He has already done it! The salvation of God delivered everything to you. Don't be anxious about the appearance when the deliverance is in His proclamation. You can afford to wait quietly because God commands the environment. He controls the elements. He rules the kings. He speaks forth light, and He knows the end of your path. He expects us to be "settled" in an unsettled world. Wait quietly because when you speak too much, you run the risk of saying something He didn't say. We are moving against the grain of the ordinary. Waiting quietly shows your confidence.

Jeremiah was the weeping prophet, yet he still understood that his tears weren't because God was frustrated. God gets angry but He never gets frustrated. When you can find a profitable perspective concerning God, you have found the "good" place for rest. To be settled doesn't make you lazy or complacent. To be settled says you understand that things are much better out of your hands.

REFLECTION:

March 11

"At once the girl hurried into the king with the request: 'I want you to give me right now the head of John the Baptist on a platter'" (Mark 6:25 New International Version).

I find it difficult to be encouraging after reading this passage of scripture. However, the Bible does tell us not to fear those who can only harm the body, and to fear Him that can destroy both soul and body in hell's fire. John's entire life was meant to be a sacrifice for the purposes of God. He was a prophet that prepared the way for the Lord. Although hers was an extremely sadistic request, John's life was in the hands of God. Your enemies think if they can vex you all of your days and then cause a horrible death, somehow God's plan is thwarted. What would the head of John the Baptist mean to her? The lives that John impacted were still impacting others.

Your legacy will continue to speak for you when you can no longer speak for yourself. The book of Genesis explains how Abel's blood cried out to God from the ground. When people remember how you lived, it doesn't matter how you die. Now that John was deceased, the ministry of Jesus exploded. John fulfilled his purpose, and God wants you to fulfill yours. Many centuries later, we are still blessed by the life and testimony of John the Baptist. John said, "He must increase and I must decrease." There is no greater love than to lay down your life for your friend. I applaud John for having the courage to take the ultimate decrease.

REFLECTION:

_____

_____

_____

_____

_____

_____

_____

March 12

"Even though you have ten thousand guardians in Christ, you do not have many fathers, for in Christ Jesus I became your father through the gospel" (I Corinthians 4:15 New International Version).

I marvel at how many people lower their standards when it comes to following a spiritual leader or finding a church. There is much more to being a good pastor than being a good preacher, or a good teacher. We go to great lengths to find a good doctor, a good mechanic, a good school, a good job, a good attorney, a good accountant, a good financial advisor, and a good spouse, but why not a good pastor? Think about it. You're planning to submit to an environment for spiritual growth and the feeding of your soul! What is more important than that? Here are a few things to consider about ministries: Who serves or served as a father or advisor to the leader? What is the Bible study like? What else goes on that can impact your life and your family? Is anything happening to be a blessing to the community? Is there a plurality of leadership or a one person show? Is the Bible the heart of the ministry? I could continue but these will do for now.

Paul didn't just plant churches; he fathered them. There are many fellowships that have started from bitterness and strife. The best way to start a fellowship is to have your mentor bless and install you, similarly to the way a father gives away the bride at a wedding. If you're in leadership without a mentor or a covering, I believe you're not functioning in the center of God's will. Do whatever it takes, so you're not a lone ranger reproducing other lone rangers.

REFLECTION:

March 13

"You shall seek those who contend with you and shall not find them; they who war against you shall be as nothing, as nothing at all" (Isaiah 41:12 Amplified Bible).

God will always be known as Israel's helper. He still comes to the aid of His faithful ones. To be faithful doesn't mean you always do everything right. To be faithful means you have been chosen to reveal His good works. As a friend of God, you must accept that you also have enemies. God has plans for them just like He has plans for you. Thank goodness His plans for them are much different. You can't possibly handle the power of your adversaries. God gives you strength to deal with the things you can deal with, and He personally handles what you can't.

Jesus said, "Without Me you can do nothing." If you examine that statement, it means you are NEVER as strong as you need to be. It's amazing that God would go to this length in order to deliver you. Your enemies won't be found anywhere. He will either subdue them to the point of making them serve you, or He will totally eliminate them. The prophet encouraged the people because they were constantly in turmoil and battle. Your life is also a constant battle. Enormous obstacles are a daily reality. HOWEVER, God has already published the blueprint for your success. You are His place of habitation, and He knows every square foot of your existence: body, soul, and spirit.

REFLECTION:

March 14

"You made men ride over our heads; we went through fire and through water, yet You brought us out into a place of abundance" (Psalms 66:12 New American Standard).

Sometimes God allows your foes to make you humble. Fire and water were the tools of judgment for the earth. God will walk close enough with you, so judgment won't harm you. God Himself will be your strength and your guide. Your enemy is larger and wiser than you, but your enemy is small and ignorant to the ways of God. Your enemy can see you, but he can't see the power behind you. Your enemy knows you, but he doesn't know the One that sent you. Make sure you don't engage him in your own strength. This verse teaches that God is the One behind victory and defeat. There is rich fulfillment waiting for you. Fulfillment can only happen at the other end of a promise.

Fire is designed to consume everything it doesn't perfect. Water is designed to saturate everything it doesn't satisfy. Don't assume God has forgotten you because your enemy is temporarily riding high. The most important aspect of your walk with God is the way you finish. I would rather start shaky and finish strong than start strong and finish shaky. God wants you to increase in favor and stature. The New Testament uses words like build, add, strengthen, exercise, and work. The idea is that you will continually abound in the plan of God. Growth is what God has planned for you in every aspect of your life. Rich fulfillment means you will enjoy the benefits of God with the presence of God.

REFLECTION:

_____

_____

_____

_____

_____

_____

March 15

"Jesus said to her, 'Did I not tell you and promise you that if you would believe and rely on Me, you should see the glory of God?'" (John 11:40 Amplified Bible).

Martha was head-driven as opposed to heart-driven. Jesus often had to reassure her repeatedly before she would stop talking long enough to know what's really happening. Martha seemed to believe that the way to a man's heart is through her work while Mary believed that the way to God's heart is through her worship. Mary often worshiped while Martha often worked. The promise of Jesus guarantees that you will see the glory of God through your power to believe.

Do you rely on Jesus more than anyone? Do you believe Him more than anything? Do you live through His faith more than your feelings? Jesus endured a lifetime as a human being so that we would learn to trust God. This verse is here as a response to the death of a loved one. Can anything rock your faith more than that? Jesus transforms those things that appear permanent into temporary things. Those dead areas in your life are still subject to whatever you expect. God talks to you through the most difficult circumstances you will ever have. Who do you talk to in your most difficult circumstances? I know I seem to be asking a lot of questions. However, I think many of you reading this realize that Jesus is probably asking the same questions.

REFLECTION:

_____

_____

_____

_____

_____

_____

_____

_____

March 16

"Now from the sixth hour there was darkness over all the land until the ninth hour" (Matthew 27:45 Revised Standard Version).

I don't think it's coincidental that Matthew chapters 26 and 27 are the longest two chapters in the book of Matthew. These two chapters describe the events that led to the suffering and death of Jesus. It must have seemed to take forever to recall and record these events. Darkness in the middle of the day tells me that even nature itself was confused and thrown off balance. Could this be the day that paradise would be restored? Is the one who holds the universe together falling apart? The earth is merely broadcasting the tug-of-war over its ownership. The first Adam gave it to Satan. Now the last Adam was taking it back. I believe the entire earth was dark.

What do you think people would say if something like this happened today? Every newscast worldwide would have a programming interruption with a special news bulletin. There are many unique aspects in the life of Jesus that should cause us to make a decision about Him. He must be more than just a great humanitarian. He must be more than just a prominent historical icon. He must be more than just a zealot for righteousness. He must be more than just a charismatic man of great persuasion. He must be more than just a timeless philosopher. He IS all of these things and then some. He is the Savior of the world, King of kings, and Lord of lords. He is God in human flesh. Amen!

REFLECTION:

March 17

"I will save you from the hands of the wicked and redeem you from the grasp of the cruel" (Jeremiah 15:21 New International Version).

This fifteenth chapter of Jeremiah is a very sobering reminder of the importance of repentance. God had declared how even if Moses and Samuel stood before Him; there would be no hope for the rebellious. Nevertheless, once again, God can't reject one who laments over their sin. I believe the goal is never to be overcome by the wicked and cruel. Our lives typically take on cycles. When things are good, our behavior is good. When things aren't so good, our behavior follows suit.

God wants to strengthen us so that He gets the same results no matter what happens. He desires that adversity yields the same praise as prosperity. It's easy to say but hard to do. The hands of the wicked are those who try to work destruction in our lives. The grasp of the cruel are those who God has given authority over you, yet they think they own you. God's redemption prevails over the plans of EVERYONE else! You may have to spend some time under cruel hands to keep you from wandering. Don't lengthen your stay. The desire of God is to establish you so others can see what He does with a willing vessel. When your heart finds Him, He finds room for you regardless of your past!

REFLECTION:

March 18

"Unless the Lord builds the house, its builders labor in vain. Unless the Lord watches over the city, the watchmen stand guard in vain" (Psalms 127:1 New International Version).

I believe many of us depend on our skills to accomplish great things. We should certainly expect to use our talents as an expression of gratitude and an investment in our future. Don't allow yourself to reach a point where you think things happen because of you. Your skills, talents, abilities, and creative concepts have a source. The existence of any structure has many contributors. Yet, all of those contributors were inspired by an all-knowing source. God involves Himself in all things that are progressive. Every victory happens because God had mercy on you.

Today's governments pride themselves on their military might. If God doesn't allow an army or navy to exhibit expertise in combat skills, that armed forces collection would be utterly defeated. God plans to wipe out the armies that surround tiny little Israel. Logic would tell you that Israel wouldn't stand a chance against opponents like Russia, China, Japan, and others, especially all at once! But, because the Lord watches over His city and His people, it doesn't matter how many attack them. God can defend you when it seems like you will be consumed. It's good to have watchmen, but it's better to have God.

REFLECTION:

March 19

"When I was in deep trouble, I searched for the Lord. All night long I pray, with hands lifted toward heaven, pleading. There can be no joy for me until he acts" (Psalms 77:2 New Living Translation).

Although we hate to admit it, we WILL have moments like this. The bible says that our days are few and full of troubles. I'm glad the psalmist knew enough to search for God and wait for Him to respond. When you depend on God, this is the only thing you can do. Some people that don't really know God try to call Him when their backs are against the wall. When He doesn't respond like they want Him to, they take other options and then slander God as though He works for them. If you don't ALWAYS need Him, you don't EVER need Him. Who can have the audacity to "decide" what God should do and when?

God is the only one with the power to either change your situation or give you peace until it changes. If it takes all night long, stay there. Sometimes we plead with God about health issues, financial issues, the salvation of a loved one, and many other things. Regardless of the outcome, God loves you. Regardless of your income, God loves you. Sometimes He answers your prayers according to your liking; sometimes He doesn't. The psalmist refused to be comforted until God involved Himself. God is faithful, and He will come through for you one way or another. Don't be so focused on your request that you miss His response.

REFLECTION:

85

March 20

"Do you see a man diligent and skillful in his business? He will stand before kings; he will not stand before obscure men" (Proverbs 22:29 Amplified Bible).

God has designed a plan for prosperity. You probably won't hear a lot about it though. Be thoroughly involved in YOUR business. Did you know that God wants you to stand before kings? He doesn't want you to serve them; He wants to make you a peer. The unbeatable combination of diligence and skill will put you in a position of strength. Obscure men have no leadership skills. It takes a certain kind of person to persevere until God makes your spiritual investments fruitful. Your job is to discover what God intends to get from your business. He has given you gifts to help you succeed in your endeavors. He has also given you alliances for your advancement. He has given you a path to travel. Since He has invested so much in you, there should be an expectation to receive from your production. Solomon knew that God was faithful, even when it didn't feel good. Solomon also had the benefit of witnessing the blessings of God in his father's life. Building your business will allow you to save, lend, store, give, and bless others. When you decide this will be your pursuit, God is obligated to accompany you.

REFLECTION:

March 21

"As He was getting into the boat, the man who had been demon-possessed was imploring Him that he might be accompany Him" (Mark 5:18 New American Standard).

This is the man that was delivered from Legion (many demonic spirits). When the demon was cast out, they caused a herd of pigs to drown in the sea. This man struggled to survive the horrors of possession until Jesus met him. Jesus didn't allow the man to go with Him, but He told him to make the Lord's compassion known in his community. The gospel of Mark doesn't take much time explaining things. The key word in Mark's gospel is "immediately." We can learn a valuable lesson from this gospel writer. This perspective of the life of Jesus tells us that the King's business requires haste. Many people thronged and crowded Him because of His healing power. Others gathered around Him because of His great wisdom, yet others were sick with jealousy and envy, and wanted to eliminate Him. What is it that attracts you to Him? It is impossible to be confronted with Him and not have any reaction whatsoever. He is the only one with universal impact. He even connected with nature in such a way that can't be denied. If you know Him, you have been freed from something, too. Some have a more dramatic testimony than others, but we all have a story to tell. Examine your life so you can decide who would best benefit from knowing what the Lord has done for you. It might surprise you to find out who would actually listen.

REFLECTION:

March 22

"For our light and momentary troubles are achieving for us an eternal glory that far outweighs them all" (II Corinthians 4:17 New Living Translation).

How many of you have more televisions in your house than members of your household? How many of you guys have more pairs of shoes than days of the week? You're probably wondering what my point is. When today's preachers don't tell you their troubles but tell you how to get through yours, it just doesn't carry much weight. Somehow adversity just can't take advice from prosperity. We must find a way to relate before we can effectively advise. Paul was familiar with having more than enough and having nowhere near enough. He was received because he went through the things his listeners were going through.

Don't think you need to have experienced everything others have gone through. But, they at least need to know you can feel compassion for their plight. Paul was an even greater encouragement because he was currently enduring, yet he was still able to exhort. How often have you visited someone in their affliction, expecting to help them, only to leave feeling like they've helped you? This is a verse of perspective. You have a greater chance of contentment in your trials when you know something better awaits you. The weight of God's glory makes the weight of your trials worth it.

REFLECTION:

March 23

"And these are but the outer fringe of his works; how faint the whisper we hear of him! Who then can understand the thunder of his power?" (Job 26:14 New International Version)

Can you actually consider the potential of omnipotence? The powerful forces of nature alone should make us bow in awe of God's abilities. He controls the rains, winds, snow, sands, oceans, asteroids, heat, and EVERYTHING else. Job talked about His ownership of the earth and all inhabitants. He said, "Death is naked before God." Jesus is the only one that ruined death's undefeated record. God can do whatever He wants. Who can you appeal to?

The things we see and experience are simply "outer fringes" of His power. It isn't possible for anyone to absorb His full magnitude. God confines Himself to measurable portions, so we don't come unglued. Even when He revealed awesome glimpses of His glory, people collapsed until He laid His hand upon them. Truly the bible is right when it tells us how He pities our frame because He knows we are just dust. God handles you very gently, even when you feel like you can't take another thing. The power of the sun affects us from a distance of 93 million miles. The power of the Son affects us from the right hand of God. Now THAT'S power.

REFLECTION:

March 24

"He who by charging excessive interest and by unjust efforts to get gain increases his material possession, gathers it for him [to spend] who is kind and generous to the poor" (Proverbs 28:8 Amplified Bible).

We are living in a society that believes strongly in the term "by any means necessary." We have witnessed predatory lending, phone scams, legal loopholes, fine print, deceptive marketing, and downright moral crimes. It may help you to realize that God keeps score regardless of who doesn't. Men find new and innovative ways to exact financial harm on their fellow man. You need a lawyer. You can't afford to interpret a contract you can't understand to purchase an item that probably isn't worth it. Greed is at epidemic proportions, so you really have to negotiate the best situation for your resources.

Solomon wrote the Proverbs, so that should tell you this is nothing new. God promises to distribute the resources of the wicked to those who will steward them in righteousness. Can you be kind and generous to the poor? Your kindness will put resources within their reach. Your generosity will cause you to treat them the same way you treat the wealthy. Jesus often mentioned how He takes personally the way you treat the poor. He puts Himself in the shoes of the underprivileged, underserved, and overlooked. God doesn't mind if you make a profit, just don't make the rich get richer at the expense of the poor.

REFLECTION:

March 25

"Fill up and complete my joy by living in harmony and being of the same mind and one in purpose, having the same love, being in full accord and of one harmonious mind and intention" (Philippians 2:2 Amplified Bible).

Paul understood that his joy wasn't dependent upon anyone else's lifestyle. Yet, he also knew that it would be fulfilling to see others living in harmony. It's completely chaotic when people that should be working together work against each other. Paul didn't have the opportunity to visit them in person so he wrote down his desires for them. These are also God's wishes for the church. How would your body look if each organ did whatever it pleased? How would your hand accomplish anything if each finger pulled in a different direction? Similarly, the church can only be a witness to the world as we work together. Adults have a hard time submitting mostly because we've waited our entire lives to make our own decisions. Rebellion is natural; submission is spiritual.

Small children aren't taught to be crafty. Pre-teens aren't instructed in deception. Teenagers don't take classes about resisting authority. No wonder we have adults that think their way is the best way or even the only way. Jesus said, "I am the way...." He didn't just say He "knows" the way; He "is" the way. Music is satisfying when notes that are completely different learn to work together. Every song ever written was composed by a creative use of just twelve possible notes. What could God accomplish with His creative use of each person in the body of Christ?

REFLECTION:

91

March 26

"They devise injustices, saying, 'We are ready with a well-conceived plot;' For the inward thought and the heart of a man are deep" (Psalms 64:6 New American Standard).

David knew that his position as king required God's help in exposing the secret plans of his enemies. When you study the outcomes of kings in the Bible, you discover that many of them were sabotaged by jealous family members. The position of king was the ultimate lust for power. When God didn't choose them, there was no lasting protection. David was chosen by God and depended on God's mercy for his long reign.

You don't ever want to function in a position God didn't ordain for you. There are many kinds of people: those who want what you have (envy); those who just don't want you to have it (jealousy); those who want you destroyed because you have it (enemies); and those who pretend they're happy for you yet add misery to your experience (foes). God keeps record of those things we consider private. When God is on your side, He causes all others to "line up" behind His purpose.

David was the last one remembered by his earthly father, yet he was the first one selected by his heavenly Father. God was at work in David's life for years before everyone else knew it. Value the private things God does for you, and He will make those things public.

REFLECTION:

March 27

"Our God approaches with the noise of thunder. Fire devours everything in his way, and a great storm rages around him" (Psalms 50:3 New Living Translation).

This is one of those verses that makes the word "awesome" come to mind. Sometimes I think we forget that God doesn't have to participate inconspicuously. He can choose to be very low-key, or He can choose to be very high profile. When God decides to take over a situation, there's no mistaking who is moving. Thunder has a way of letting you know that something spectacular is happening. Yet, thunder will be the preview of His arrival. God's presence can cause what the book of Peter refers to as FERVENT heat. Lava is molten rock; the center of the earth is debated to be anywhere from 3000 to 100,000 degrees CELCIUS!

Everything about God is unfathomable, but we still have the audacity to treat Him in common ways. Who has any right to complain to Him? He has given us the privilege of a relationship with Him. Most of us live as though He really doesn't have the right to insist that we do anything. If God didn't veil His glory and His majesty, we would literally dissolve because of His purity and splendor. We have become so accustomed to God moving in secret that He is often ignored and seldom considered. One thing is for sure: His involvement always has permanent impact. When He moves in the above manner, the universe will be thoroughly impressed!

REFLECTION:

March 28

"People who are at ease mock those in trouble. They give a push to people who are stumbling" (Job 12:5 New Living Translation).

Even with everything Job went through, he couldn't even count on his "friends" for compassion. If you are going to go through the trouble of visiting someone in their calamity, please don't waste valuable time trying to figure out why God allowed it. If God sent you, go as an ambassador of compassion. If God wanted to punish them, why would He send help? When God really does reveal His will, great anguish and great revelation will take place. We will all discover that we aren't as smart as we thought.

Many of those who are supposed to be shepherds only make you feel bad because you haven't been bountifully blessed. Is it because you don't tithe? Is it because you don't sow into everyone's good ground? Isn't your ground good too if Jesus is your Lord? Job's only weakness was that God was bragging about him. The only difference in anyone's life is the grace of God. The successful haven't found a SECRET to success. God says, "I will be gracious to whom I will be gracious." The mockers and pushers should be very careful because we reap what we sow. If it's springtime in your life right now, don't snub someone else going through a spiritual blizzard. When you push someone who is stumbling, you're responsible for their fall.

REFLECTION:

March 29

"However, I consider my life worth nothing to me, if only I may finish the race and complete the task the Lord Jesus has given me—the task of testifying to the gospel of God's grace" (Acts 20:24 New International Version).

We know that Paul finished his course well from the writings of 2 Timothy. This verse tells us that he made his mind up early in his walk. God warned Paul about the suffering that would come in his life. We admire Paul because of His calling and anointing, but we often forget how much he really suffered. He was stoned, shipwrecked, beaten, exposed to the elements, tortured, imprisoned, and abandoned by practically every comrade. After all these things, his only mission remained declaring the GRACE of God.

Paul didn't have low self-esteem or some inferiority complex. He knew his life meant nothing as long as he was in control of it. Your life has great worth to God, and your earthly significance increases dramatically when God is in charge. Paul was preparing to leave on another gospel journey. He had to focus on his calling to be able to face the unknown trials ahead of him. You face unknown trials everyday also, and each day is another step on your journey. Make up your mind that you will finish your course, too. Everyone's life includes a measure of suffering. Position yourself so you can continue to see grace regardless of your circumstances.

REFLECTION:

March 30

"But I have this against you, that you tolerate the woman Jezebel, who calls herself a prophetess, and she teaches and leads My bond-servants astray, so that they commit acts of immorality and eat things sacrificed to idols." (Revelation 2:20 New American Standard)

This is part of the message Jesus gives to the church at Thyatira. This message is very similar to the one given to Pergamum. Jesus gave a previous rebuke for allowing the teachings of Balaam. It could be that because Balaam was a prophet that his error is now being taken to a new level by the Jezebel spirit. This is one reason why sound doctrine is extremely important. If you don't know the foundation of what you're being taught, someone "charming" and intelligent can lead you astray.

Lucifer/Satan himself is described as "full of wisdom and perfect in beauty." It should be impossible for wolves in sheep's clothing to reach a place of leadership in the church of Jesus Christ. One of the roles of Elders in the early church was to protect the flock and expose grievous wolves. Unfortunately, we have given more credence to a degree and a business plan than the word and prayer. Yes...I know......these things are important; but do they have to be MORE important? The church is loaded with intelligent, flesh-driven success managers. We need more people who can tell the difference between the Holy Spirit and the psychic hotline. He who has an ear, let him hear what the Spirit says to the churches.

REFLECTION:

March 31

"The slave-girl therefore who kept the door said to Peter, 'You are not also one of this man's disciples, are you?' He said, 'I am not'" (John 18:17 New American Standard).

When the pressure squeezes you, one of two things will happen. You will produce a refreshing scent or a repugnant stench. Proverbs tells us that fainting in the day of adversity makes you a person of small strength. Peter often responded admirably to confrontation as long as Jesus was near. This occasion wasn't exactly one of Peter's shining moments. We have all had times where we fell short of the goal. A young girl challenged Peter's convictions of loyalty by asking a simple question. There are very few of us who would have the courage to subject ourselves to the treatment Jesus received.

Peter denied any association with Jesus because he felt completely alone. A combination of the right factors will expose human vulnerability. Examine yourself and be honest about your weaknesses. What good is it to know everyone else's weaknesses except yours? I find it rather compelling that a slave-girl would speak up to Peter. The enemy gets extremely bold when it looks like your help is nowhere near. Peter was asked two more times if he was a follower of Jesus. He vehemently denied it and felt the conviction of God in his heart. Jesus restored him, and Jesus will restore you too when your heart is right.

REFLECTION:

APRIL

April 1

"I am the Lord your God, who brought you up out of the land of Egypt. Open your mouth wide, and I will fill it" (Psalms 81:10 English Standard Version).

This is one of those times when it is perfectly alright to have a big mouth. The scripture teaches that your mouth reveals the abundance of your heart. When your heart is fixed on the fact that God delivered you from the bondage of sin, then your mouth will only confirm the greatness of your God. Do you believe that a person speaks fondly concerning whatever they feel fondly about? Athletes discuss athletics; artists discuss art. Musicians discuss music, so what about Christians? How do you "feel" about the Lord your God? Do you know that He delivered you from death row?

Until you have a personal relationship with Christ, you are a walking corpse. I know that sounds rather graphic. It may even sound like some science fiction exaggeration, but it is the Bible truth. God says He wants to fill your mouth. When He fills it, only what He puts in will come out. He will give you wisdom, discretion, knowledge, encouragement, and self-control. I will take the liberty of assuming that you also have said many things you are still regretting. This psalm speaks volumes about the redemptive work of God. Governing your speech and supplying you with verbal substance is only a small portion of your Christian perks.

REFLECTION:

_____

_____

_____

_____

_____

_____

_____

April 2

"Do not rejoice when your enemy falls, and do not let your heart be glad when he stumbles" (Proverbs 24:17 New American Standard).

God has never been in favor of gloating when your enemy falls on hard times. If God expects to feed you in the presence of your enemies, why should He expect you to be concerned with what's happening with them? God wants you to watch your own behavior, not anyone else's. An enemy is someone who makes it their business to hinder your progress. An enemy hates you without cause. Be careful because some people hate the fact that God delights in showing you favor. Solomon never really concerned himself with how God treated his enemies. There will certainly be resistance to what God intends for you.

The resistance you encounter is no indication that God has forgotten you. Solomon also had the benefit of being a second-generation king. God promised to bless the seed of David, so there was a benefit in being David's offspring. Wait for God to fulfill His purposes in your life. Regardless of what happens with anyone else, there is an expectation that God will honor His word to you. Your service won't be in vain. Your faith won't be in vain. Your labor won't be in vain, and your sowing won't be in vain.

REFLECTION:

April 3

"On this mountain the Lord Almighty will prepare a feast of rich food for all peoples, a banquet of aged wine—the best of meats and the finest of wines" (Isaiah 25:6 New International Version).

God has a special liking for mountains. A mountain is symbolic of rising above your circumstances and situations. A mountain is also symbolic of a challenge. A mountain can even typify new levels of aspiration. In any event, God wants to make His mountain a place of fellowship and celebration. God has always wanted to be everyone's God. He intends to be a blessing to every nation, kindred, and people. Sometimes we think God is playing favorites. God doesn't choose you in order to be exclusive. He chose you so that you would be a channel of blessing for EVERYONE in your sphere of influence. God has reserved the best for you. A feast of rich food and a banquet of aged wine tell us that He has spared no expense.

In the giving of His Son, He has gone to the greatest extent of His reserves. What does your heart tell you when you see the things God has done for you? God could very easily have done away with all of us and started all over again. Yet, His grace and mercy have caused Him to enter into covenant. The promise of God has obligated Him to perform according to your need. If He responded according to your performance, you would be consumed! The plan of God will be fulfilled without denial. His plan will be fulfilled without delay. His plan will be fulfilled without defeat, and His plan will be fulfilled without derailment.

REFLECTION:

April 4

"He said, 'In my distress I called to the Lord, and he answered me. From the depths of the grave I called for help, and you listened to my cry'" (Jonah 2:2 New International Version).

Listening to Jonah's prayer, you would think he was being chased by an enemy, or maybe a victim of circumstance. Well, I guess he was a victim of his own circumstance. Before you bash Jonah, ask yourself how many times have you traveled in the opposite direction of God's clear instruction and prayed for deliverance? The book of Jonah really isn't about Jonah. It mentions Jonah but it reveals God. In fact, the entire Bible mentions people, angels, demons, and lots of events in an attempt to attract us to a relationship with God through Jesus Christ.

God came to Jonah's rescue because it would glorify Him to do so. The gospel needed to get to the Ninevites, so they could repent of their atrocities. The plan God has for you won't be denied by any earthly force, heavenly occupant, or even your own stubbornness. You might say that God loves you enough to chastise you into repentance just so He can forgive you AGAIN and allow you to complete the mission He called you for. No wonder the Bible says that the love of God passes knowledge. Your decisions pave the road to your destiny. Sometimes you take a detour on the road; but you will still be guided home.

REFLECTION:

April 5

"And behold, the angel of the Lord came upon him, and a light shined in the prison: and he smote Peter on the side, and raised him up, saying, Arise up quickly. And his chains fell off from his hands" (Acts 12:7 King James Version).

The arrest of Peter happened during a heightened period of persecution in the church. James had just been martyred, and Herod apparently had similar plans for Peter because the Jews consented to the death of James. I wonder how many members a persecuted church would have today? You never know what plans God has for you. Peter had to be thinking that his time was up, too. The book of Acts takes a turn at this point to the ministries of Paul and Barnabas. There wasn't too much more said about Peter, which raises the question: why did God deliver him from prison? Personally, I believe God delivered him to encourage the baby Christians that were praying for him. It may have broken their hearts if Peter had been executed at that time.

If you look back at the passage, the Bible said they were "earnestly" praying for him. It would be just like our compassionate God to answer their prayers even though the ministry of Peter wasn't going to be very prominent. Peter could have written his letters from prison at any time. Actually, the tendency to write usually happens when you don't have time for much else. The angel took Peter to those who were praying, and they enjoyed a glorious reunion amidst great affliction. God knows how to use you for His greatest glory.

REFLECTION:

April 6

"'Neither,' he replied, 'but as commander of the army of the Lord I have now come.' Then Joshua fell face down to the ground in reverence, and asked him, 'What message does my Lord have for his servant?'" (Joshua 5:14 New International Version).

This "Man" appeared to Joshua with a sword drawn in His hand. Joshua wanted to know whose side He was on. Have you noticed how God really doesn't take sides? God gives you favor when you side with Him. Many of us would have been alarmed to find that He was for neither side. The commander of the Lord's host came to advance the will of God on earth. The same thing is still happening today. Angels are ministering spirits sent forth to steward God's will. Joshua had the right response when he realized what was happening. God will show up at the right time when you're facing your biggest challenges and major battles. There is a very valuable lesson here. No matter how well you have drawn up the plan, your first question must always be, "What message does the Lord have for me?"

Victory will never depend on your skill and preparation as much as your submission and obedience. We should certainly plan and prepare but allow God to guide you in the implementation process. Joshua was victorious because he was chosen. Joshua spent years watching God work in the life of Moses. Joshua's confidence was no longer based on the life of Moses; it was now based on the faithfulness of God. There are times in your life as a leader when God deals directly with you, instead of indirectly through others.

REFLECTION:

April 7

"Now therefore come, proclaim in the hearing of the people, saying, 'Whoever is afraid and trembling, let him return and depart from Mount Gilead.' So, 22,000 people returned, but 10,000 remained" (Judges 7:3 New American Standard).

This is no time for the fearful and afraid. At least they didn't pretend they were courageous. What could be worse than expecting someone to cover you, only to discover they are paralyzed with fear when you need them? When you're able to admit your condition, you have taken the most difficult step toward recovery. Gideon was already greatly outnumbered, so he had to be concerned when 2/3 of his army departed. This verse doesn't mention the fact that this group was reduced even more. By the time God was finished proving them, there remained only 300 soldiers. I'm sure there was a great surprise when the fearful ones were exposed. Many were physically intimidating men of great stature. Some were probably highly skilled strategists. Some were no doubt familiar with the territory and may have even been instrumenta in previous victories. These were some of the reasons God disqualified them for this battle.

You will sometimes find yourself in situations that are impossible. God wouldn't put you in an impossible situation unless He planned to beat impossible odds. Even when God comes to your aid, you still must fight. Don't expect things to be a walk in the park. Do your best and He will make up the difference.

REFLECTION:

April 8

"When he heard that it was Jesus of Nazareth, he began to shout, "Jesus, Son of David, have mercy on me" (Mark 10:47 New International Version).

Bartimaeus was sitting on the roadside begging when he heard that Jesus was in the vicinity. Do you start thinking about what you need when Jesus is near, or do you start thinking about what you want? Bartimaeus was blind; he wasn't concerned with the luxuries of life. He shouted even louder after some in the crowd began to rebuke him. His need outweighed his reputation. His need exceeded his image to the crowd.

Until you pursue your needs more than your desires, you will flounder in the things of God. This man got the attention of Jesus after he got the attention of the crowd. I find it interesting that Jesus didn't address him until he cried louder. We must learn how to overcome obstacles, press through resistance, and even continue against popular opinion if we expect to take advantage of God's presence. Your life will back you into corners that only a shout can get you out of. Don't be so dignified that you miss the chance of a lifetime. It's okay if you have to endure a little embarrassment for the cause of Christ. Since Christ hung naked on the cross as a public spectacle for hours for you, can you shout your need for Him for just a few seconds?

REFLECTION:

April 9

"How much more, then, will the blood of Christ, who through the eternal Spirit, offered himself unblemished to God, cleanse our consciences from acts that lead to death, so that we may serve the living God" (Hebrews 9:14 New International Version).

In the book of Hebrews, God exalts Jesus just like He promised He would in the book of Philippians. There were many times in the Old Testament where Jesus was kept in the shadows. The sacrifices of bulls, goats, doves, and more pointed to the coming of Christ. God instituted the sacrificial system because He knew there was a "better" way coming. The blood of those sacrifices temporarily dealt with human issues, but the blood of Jesus permanently dealt with eternal issues.

The New Testament has once again raised the bar from dealing with conduct to dealing with conscience. God knows if we think properly, we will act properly. To serve the living God requires that we give ourselves as an unblemished blood sacrifice. No other blood sacrifice was willing. Every animal was brought to the priest to be slain on the altar. Jesus, like Isaac, could have resisted, yet He willingly offered Himself and submitted to the will of His Father. Because of Him, we can come as living sacrifices and take advantage of the power to serve and please God.

REFLECTION:

April 10

"What you ought to say is, 'If the Lord wants us to, we will live and do this or that'" (James 4:15 New Living Translation).

We make plans for the moment, plans for the hour, plans for the day, plans for the week, plans for the year, and plans for a lifetime. Most of us don't deliberately assume we'll be around. Is this verse chastising us for not remembering that nothing is promised? I'll let you answer that question. If you're anything like me, sometimes this verse comes to mind when I say things like "I'll see you tomorrow." This verse is in the bible for a reason. There was a person in the Bible that made plans without considering God, and God called him a FOOL. He wasn't a fool because he didn't know he would die that night; he was a fool because he was selfish and didn't even consider what God wanted from his life.

Try your best to govern your conversation with scripture in mind. There's nothing wrong with saying what you "plan" to do. I like to say things like "if nothing happens I'll be there." I don't always remember, but at least consideration is given. One thing is for sure, when God gave His people instructions about "tomorrow," that was a guarantee they would be around. Things happen suddenly in this life, and we need to consider our words and choose them carefully. I think this verse is probably a caution against careless speech and assumptive conclusions. We need continuous and periodic reminders about how much we depend on God. It is truly in Him that we live, move, and have our being.

REFLECTION:

April 11

"But seeing the wind, he became frightened, and beginning to sink, he cried out, 'Lord, save me'" (Matthew 14:30 New American Standard).

Well, let's see now. I know we've all heard this passage preached from the standpoint: "Peter took his eyes off of Jesus." Those of you who really know me realize this isn't quite enough for me. Peter was rebuked for his doubt. What did he doubt? Apparently, he doubted whether the person walking toward him was Jesus. NEVER let what you "see" cause doubt about what you "heard." Faith comes by hearing and hearing by the Word. There are many times in life where we will have to come out of our comfort "boats." Sinking in your circumstances shouldn't make you doubt it was God that called you. We are told that we walk by FAITH and not by SIGHT! This is a beautiful account of how God wants us to respond to His word without worrying about the environment that His word takes us through. Nothing in this passage says the wind became boisterous AFTER he got out of the boat.

Why should our circumstances shake our confidence in God? Does your circumstance shape your concept of God? Peter walked on the water because he believed, by faith, that Jesus said so. Believe me, God WILL call you into perilous waters! Yet, when your confidence remains in the One who called you, you too can walk on water (don't try this at home). Anyway, even the sinking was part of Jesus' plan to make Peter continue the faith-walk. Even when you're afraid, the desperation cry of "Lord save me" will reestablish your faith in Jesus.

REFLECTION:

109

April 12

"With a view to this we toil and strive, [yes] and suffer reproach, because we have [fixed our] hope on the living God, Who is the Savior (Preserver, Maintainer, Deliverer) of all men, especially of those who believe—trust in, rely on and adhere to Him" (I Timothy 4:10 Amplified Bible).

Are you more concerned with your reputation or your destination? This verse must be carefully examined, or you might really think EVERYONE is saved. Yes, Jesus is Lord. He doesn't "become" Lord when you agree with His majesty. And yes, He is the Savior of the whole world. Wait a minute...what I mean is that He is the only hope of salvation for the world. He takes care of everyone: including His enemies. Once again, He doesn't "become" Savior when you agree with who He is. How many times does He say, "I AM?" I don't remember Him saying "I become."

When you accept Jesus' atonement for your sin, God adopts you as a son in relationship, not just as a human product of His creativity. The creation is waiting for deliverance, too. Restoration must come to everything, not just humanity. The earth was the womb that produced Adam. God made man from the dust of the ground and gave him dominion; therefore, the fall of Adam affected everything. Because of the importance of your destination, you strive, toil, and suffer reproach, ridicule, and pain. When you believe in God, you must also believe God. The bowing of your will signifies your submission. You can't lead sometimes and follow sometimes when it comes to God. He ALWAYS leads, and you ALWAYS follow.

REFLECTION:

April 13

"From the end of the earth   call to You when my heart is faint; lead me to the rock that is higher than I" (Psalms 61:2 New American Standard).

Your life will be filled with struggles, battles, trials, and tests. Victory is sweeter when you remember the pain of defeat. God is never out of reach. He will respond when you call. You won't always like His response though. You will be challenged to know the difference between pruning and punishment. If you have peace in your trial, you are being pruned. If you have no peace in your trial, you are being punished. God knows what to do in order to get you to the high Rock. You have to find a way to connect with Jesus regardless of the reason for your calamity.

If your heart is faint, you need refreshing. You can get water, encouragement, perspective instruction, direction, and strength from the Rock. Call on the Lord when you get weary. Call on the Lord when you get overwhelmed. Call on the Lord when your adversaries seem to be advancing. Call on the Lord when you think everything is fine. If you make it a practice to call on Him at all times, your mind will stay focused on Him. The psalmist knew that God was his only hope. God has anointed you for great things, but those things can only be accomplished as you rely upon Him. He will establish your works on the same Rock He leads you to. That Rock is JESUS!

REFLECTION:

April 14

"For I reckon that the sufferings of this present time are not worthy to be compared with the glory which shall be revealed in us" (Romans 8:18 King James Version).

Is anyone discouraged? Is anyone exhausted? Is anyone frustrated? Do your enemies always seem to have the upper hand? Are you struggling with sickness? Is despair your bedfellow? Does it ALWAYS seem to be nighttime? Is your season typically "next" season? Do you have more questions than answers? Are your hopes blurred by your tears? Well, let me remind you that whatever this life throws at you doesn't deserve the same attention as what God has promised you. Everything contrary to the promise of God belongs in the category of suffering. What glory will be revealed in you? Christ in you is the hope of glory. Paul tells us that the brightness of the glory of Christ will destroy the spirit of antichrist. The anointing in you is a revelation of the "glory" of God that destroys the yoke of bondage.

When God's presence rises up in you, the glory of God is preeminent. People that always thought you would finish last will stand in awe of the God that promotes you. Jesus said, "It is finished" so that you would never have to say, "I am finished!" The Spirit of God is the "wind" beneath your wings and the "wind" behind your sails. The courage of God propels you forward into new discoveries and horizons. The sun will never set on your favor because God is the light of your new city. Many things will be revealed in you that proclaim the glory of God. Get accustomed to winning because God is carrying you by His power.

REFLECTION:

_____

_____

_____

_____

_____

_____

April 15

"May He grant you out of the riches of His glory, to be strengthened *and* spiritually energized with power through His Spirit in your inner self, [indwelling your innermost being and personality]" (Ephesians 3:16 Amplified Bible).

God has a rich and unlimited treasury at your disposal. He has given you access and authority to feed your spiritual appetite. You can only be strengthened as you partake Access without consumption is torture. If He only allows you an entrance, that would be no better than window shopping. He grants you full participation in everything that belongs to Him. That's why you are referred to as an heir of God and a joint-heir with Jesus Christ. Reinforcement allows you to go further than you think, carry more than you believed you were able, and even encourage someone else who is empty. Reinforcement is like the saucer under your cup.

There is a place in God where you can find the stability to fight inner battles. You are supported by God Himself and His glory. The Spirit of the Lord has chosen you for His habitation. When He decided to make you a new creation in Christ, there was a change in your entire structure. You look the same on the outside, but the inner man is completely different. The One who owns you has given you a new nature with new motives, new expressions, new distinctions, new tendencies, new expectations, a new temperament, and a new direction. I believe the verse is correct when it says God indwells even your personality.

REFLECTION:

April 16

"I am not saying this because I am in need, for I have learned to be content whatever the circumstances" (Philippians 4:11 New International Version).

I want to use a number of scriptures in order to make a point. I won't mention the verses; I'll just paraphrase some of them. My thoughts are not your thoughts, neither are your ways My ways. You have been bought with a price, and you are not your own. Your steps are ordered by the Lord. I will be gracious to whom I will be gracious. In Him we live, move, and have our being. You are complete in Him. I will guide you with My eyes. You have not chosen Me: I have chosen you. Father, forgive them, for they know not what they do. The hairs of your head are numbered. Take no thought for tomorrow. I love you with an everlasting love. I will restore the years the locust has eaten. For we KNOW that all things work together for good to them that love God.

Since all of these things are true, wherever you are is no accident. Whatever is going on in your life is no surprise. Although your decisions have led you to this point, God won't leave you where you are. If you're being chastised, the purpose is to prove God's love for you. If you're being challenged, the purpose is to prove your love for Him. Contentment must be learned! Contentment is impossible until trust is in place. God can satisfy every longing of the soul. Are we giving God what He longs to see from our lives?

REFLECTION:

April 17

"Only keep me in mind when it goes well with you, and please do me a kindness by mentioning me to Pharaoh, and get me out of this house" (Genesis 40:14 New American Standard).

The "house" that Joseph was referring to was a prison. God used Joseph to interpret the dreams of two of Pharaoh's servants. The chief butler (cupbearer) got a favorable interpretation. The events happened just as Joseph said they would, and the servant that was restored to his position forgot Joseph. There was no "logical" reason for Joseph to be locked up. He was falsely accused of making advances towards Potiphar's wife.

Do you examine your life and think, *I haven't done anything to deserve this prison.* Joseph was a model servant, citizen, brother, friend, and trustee. Yet, he had to wait many years before God placed him in the strategic office planned for him. We aren't told anything about Joseph's shortcomings. Nothing in the scripture reveals a rational reason for him to suffer so much. The hardness he endured never diminished his attitude toward God. Even the horrific trials of Job didn't cause him to be angry with God either. Many people today get upset with God because He allows difficult circumstances. There's nothing wrong with wanting to be released from the prison, just make sure you are completely rehabilitated.

REFLECTION:

April 18

"What was from the beginning, what we have heard, what we have seen with our eyes, what we have looked at and touched with our hands, concerning the Word of life" (I John 1:1 New American Standard).

I am about to say something extremely controversial and unpopular in today's charismatic circles. This verse outlines the essential elements of **_TRUE_** apostleship. I guess what we have running around today are either false apostles, or apostles with a small 'a'. If we can have gods with a small 'g,' why can't we have apostles with a small 'a'? The prerequisites for biblical apostleship are that you MUST have seen, looked upon, and encountered the human resurrected Christ. These qualifying elements allowed Paul to declare that He was an apostle born out of due time. He literally encountered the glorified Christ.

If you want to be addressed by the title of apostle, I will cooperate with your wishes and address you in that manner. My prayer is that you are correct in your insistence. Why is it that no one even dared claiming to be an apostle until about the last 20 years or so? I have the courage to say that it is because the criteria for qualification made it impossible for anyone to make such a claim, but now we have people that don't even mind claiming to be the Savior. Since God isn't nervous about it, I'm not either. People today need new titles to "wow" you into respect and submission. Jesus let His works speak louder than His title. I think we should follow the same example.

REFLECTION:

April 19

"This is the day which the Lord hath made; we will rejoice and be glad in it" (Psalms 118:24 King James Version).

This verse is the foundation for one of the most popular praise songs in church history. I wonder if we know how important it is to carry this mindset into each day. Every day is a gift from God to us. There will be some days that include heartache, tragedy, and other unfortunate circumstances. However, God is still able to carry us safely through each turn. Why does the writer say "we" will rejoice?

Anyone who understands the magnitude of waking up every day constitutes "we." If you knew God granted you mercy to open your eyes, the only fitting response is to rejoice. We may not be happy about everything that happens today but take the earliest opportunity to be glad that you were included in God's plans for it. There are many battles that await the child of God. The morning is the best time to prepare for the unknown events of the day. Fortify your mind. Establish your walk. Go with the intent to win. At the end of each day, go to God and recap the happenings of the day. When you start your day with God and end your day with Him, the things in between won't separate you.

REFLECTION:

April 20

"And they commanded the people, saying, 'When you see the ark of the covenant of the Lord your God with the Levitical priests carrying it, then you shall set out from your place and go after it'" (Joshua 3:3 New American Standard).

Even though some people are natural leaders, you still don't qualify to lead God's people until you have been a good follower. We need to follow directions, follow the scope of God's calling, and follow the example of godly leadership. The Proverbs tell us that God will direct our path when we seek Him in all of our ways. God has designated a certain group to bear the ark and minister to Him. He has still called certain individuals to minister to Him and equip His people.

Every child of God has a role and a part to play in the enrichment of the kingdom. We should always seek the presence of God and look for opportunities to move with Him. The scriptures tell us to seek God, hunger and thirst after God, and desire the sincere milk of the word for growth. When God moves, you move. Never mind your comfort zone or the path of popularity. The above verse commands the people of God to go after Him! Sometimes it will be daytime; sometimes it will be nighttime. Sometimes it will be popular; other times it will be unpopular. God knows how to lead His people. God knows your heart, and He expects you to follow your heart and not your head.

REFLECTION:

April 21

"For [simply] consider your own call, brethren; not many [of you were considered to be] wise, according to human estimates and standards; not many influential and powerful; not many of high and noble birth" (I Corinthians 1:26 Amplified Bible).

It's astounding how far we've fallen from depending on the Spirit of God. Education is now more important than anointing. Charisma is now more important than character. Marketing is now more important than shepherding. Thankfully, this isn't the case everywhere, but more often than not, the people of God fall into human measurements for divine standards. I saw an assessment that was based on choosing a pastor from the twelve disciples. When all factors were considered, by today's standards, Judas would have scored the highest.

When will we realize God doesn't function like we do? How can anyone take credit for their own influence? God says that He will not share His glory with anyone. We are supposed to honor those He has used, but glory belongs only to God. If we're not careful, we can think God "owes" us something for the hard work and preparation we've made. Everything God "owed" you was absorbed by Christ. Be glad He didn't give you the paycheck you earned. God uses you more when you REALLY know you shouldn't be His first option. Think about it: Anyone besides God doing the work of God is a tremendous downgrade.

REFLECTION:

April 22

"[This mystery] was never disclosed to human beings in past generations as it has now been revealed to His holy apostles [consecrated messengers] and prophets by the (Holy) Spirit" (Ephesians 3:5 Amplified Bible).

What are some of the mysteries Paul was talking about? The mystery of the New Testament and dispensation. The mystery of "Christ in you: the hope of glory." The mystery that God would deposit His Spirit in an earthen vessel. The mystery that speaks of unparalleled divine fellowship never experienced before. The mystery that God would continue to reveal Himself in new ways and means. The mystery that you can live through tribulation and be in the center of God's will. The mystery that God wanted to use Christ to eliminate animosity between nations.

We often look at people in Job-like circumstances and think God must be mad at them. But just like Job, God does mysterious things in people He considers upright. Paul considered himself to be "less than the least," otherwise he would have fallen victim to the barrage of enemy fire. I believe God is still using some people by revelation today. Revelation is different than inspiration. Your inspiration requires an "object" to pull creativity out of you; revelation comes while you are not thinking about anything in particular. God is ALWAYS the source of revelation.

REFLECTION:

April 23

"Satan, the god of this evil world, has blinded the minds of those who don't believe, so they are unable to see the glorious light of the Good News that is shining upon them. They don't understand the message we preach about the glory of Christ, who is the exact likeness of God" (II Corinthians 4:4 New Living Translation).

This verse explains, in vivid detail, the darkness we encounter on a daily basis. Sometimes I think we expect more than people are capable of giving. If a person is an unbeliever, they exist under the blinding influence of the father of lies. Only the effectual working of God's power can change their minds. When Jesus was in the world, He was the light of the world. When He left the world, He left us here as lights that should carry the gospel message. The gospel continues to shine around this evil world. God had mercy on you, so don't think He can't have mercy on others. He is counting on us to allow light, share light, and spread light.

We usually only want to be a light when we're around other lights. What good is a light around other lights? A light is most needed in a dark place. God has a plan for everyone; the only question is whether or not everyone is interested in His plan. There are lots of trappings in this world that can keep a person occupied for the rest of their lives. We must help them understand that this world is perishing, so any hope in this world is perishing, too. If you're convinced this world's system has the answer to your ills, you need a second opinion.

REFLECTION:

April 24

"The fear of the LORD is hatred of evil. Pride and arrogance and the way of evil and perverted speech I hate" (Proverbs 8:13 Revised Standard Version).

As followers of God, we must constantly ask ourselves if we share His sentiments concerning evil. We can't say we love God unless we genuinely hate the things He hates. If we don't love what He loves and hate what He hates, we are merely fooling ourselves. The respect for God will compel us to take a stand against all wrongdoing, no matter how common or popular it may be. This verse makes a distinction between pride and arrogance. One difference could be how pride makes you think you are more than you really are while arrogance makes you think others are less than they really are. Evil is a very broad category, so we have to get our perspective from the scriptures. Anything that doesn't bring glory to God would certainly fit this broad category.

Sickness wouldn't always fit this category because we don't choose sickness, and God can get glory from our infirmities. Therefore, evil seems to involve our selections more than our infections! The tree of the knowledge of good and evil is what first caused the release of evil into the world. When Adam "chose" evil, God allowed the repercussions of his choice to unfold. Whenever we say things God didn't say, we are guilty of perverted speech. When we twist divine words, we are vulnerable to a twisted perspective that doesn't come from God. He hates it when we twist His words.

REFLECTION:

_____

_____

_____

_____

_____

_____

April 25

"This is the message we have heard from him and proclaim to you, that God is light, and in him is no darkness at all" (I John 1:5 English Standard Version).

John makes a point in his general letters and in his gospel message that God is light, and Jesus is light. It is important for anyone who purposes to represent God to realize this divine attribute. Light overcomes darkness; it exposes flaws. Light causes color. Light gives direction. Light travels and moves. Light inspires awe. Light warms. Light gives heat and purifies. There is no darkness AT ALL in God. This means He is incapable of weakness; He is invulnerable. He cannot be victimized or succumb to any sort of temptation. That message was important enough for John to proclaim. I find it interesting that glory is usually described as unquenchable light.

Light can also symbolize truth since we are encouraged to walk in the light. Light could also mean honesty because nothing is hidden. We normally see light as having a source like the sun or some other star. The light of God is God Himself. Jesus called Himself the light of the world. He then also passed that description to His followers. We can never be the kind of light God is, but we can emulate His example as best we can. We should be people of truth, people who lead, people who overcome, and people who give an example worthy of following.

REFLECTION:

April 26

"Therefore, be patient, brethren, until the coming of the Lord. The farmer waits for the precious produce of the soil, being patient about it, until it gets the early and late rains" (James 5:7 New American Standard).

James is trying to encourage those who must watch the rich gorge themselves at the expense of the poor. When we constantly behold blatant injustice, the tendency is to get fed up and look for ways to take matters into our own hands. Sometimes we may even wonder if God cares or not. James reassures us that God may not be moving in a manner that's obvious to you, but He IS still moving. Don't intrude on the work of God because He isn't solving things to your satisfaction or speed. This verse mentions early and late rains. There is a time in between that looks like nothing is happening. You must know that God is NEVER idle. When you can't see what He's doing, that means He's doing something you can't see.

Just like the farmer, you have to wait for the entire process to work. What would happen if the farmer dug up his product in the middle of the season? God has promised to come back and deal with everything that goes against His word. The best thing you can do is trust Him to handle His business. The worst thing you can do is believe you can handle His business. James learned patience from walking with Jesus. Patience only comes as your faith is tried and tested. If anyone plans to follow Christ, He says you must deny yourself. That means you have to accept His methods and procedures. After denying yourself, there's a cross for you to bear. Then, you are qualified to follow Him.

REFLECTION:

April 27

"Since then, the children share in flesh and blood, He Himself likewise also partook of the same, that through death He might render powerless him who had the power of death, that is, the devil" (Hebrews 2:14 New American Standard).

Uniforms tell us a number of things. A uniform is a way of distinguishing who has been appointed to serve and help you. For example, those in a supermarket or place of business would be in uniform. A uniform is also a way of identifying whether you are dealing with a friend or foe in a military context. Jesus put on the "uniform" of flesh and blood so He could relate to everything we would encounter and to prove that He is the One who came to help you. Just think, since He defeated the devil as a man, He will annihilate him as God! It should give us great consolation and hope to know that the power of death has been destroyed. Even in Christians, the mere thought of death still causes stress and psychological implications, if we don't view it properly. Jesus came to give us a new outlook on life, as well as a new perspective on death.

Don't fall into the trap of focusing on your present condition; live in the anticipation of dwelling in your future position. Any good father wants to really understand what his children go through. Therefore, God, as our good Father, wanted to demonstrate His love by literally walking in our shoes.

REFLECTION:

April 28

"The king answered Daniel and said, 'Surely your God is a God of gods and a Lord of kings and a revealer of mysteries, since you have been able to reveal this mystery'" (Daniel 2:47 New American Standard).

At first glance, this looks like a convincing argument that Nebuchadnezzar was humbled by the awesome God of heaven. That's probably why you should take a second glance. The king was actually just impressed. There is some scriptural evidence. In verse 37, Daniel called Nebuchadnezzar "a" king of kings but also explained that the God of heaven GAVE him his power. Apparently, he forgot about that part because he put himself on God's level by calling him "a" God of Gods and not "the" God of all. That may seem trivial, but there's more. God is more than just a revealer of mysteries; He is the source of all knowledge and wisdom.

The king only saw Him as the best among other performers. He is utterly distinct in all of His ways. He is not to be compared to ANYONE! Finally, when the king walked on his balcony admiring the kingdom he had charge over, he took the credit and became a madman for a season. Would that have happened if he was humble? Make sure you don't ever forget who God really is, not just who you think He is. If you're not careful, you will believe He needs to "perform" for you in order to deserve your worship. God decided to prove Himself in Christ. If that doesn't activate your soul's search for Him, NOTHING else will!

REFLECTION:

April 29

"But on that day I will set apart the land of Goshen, where My people are living, so that no swarms of insects will be there, in order that you may know that I, the Lord, am in the midst of the land" (Exodus 8:22 New American Standard).

The magicians of Pharaoh were able to copy the signs of God through Moses and Aaron. The enemy always needs a reference point for his trickery. God is an innovator while Satan is only an imitator. God allowed these magicians to pretend as though they were really doing something. But now, God is beginning to separate Himself from any other power. Pharaoh's power was ordained through God. Any power on earth began as permission from heaven. God knows where you live; and He will protect you through all plagues. God is the Father of nature itself. He shows great signs and wonders in your life on a regular basis.

Regardless of who occupies the earthly thrones; God has established His sovereignty. There is a day coming when God will reveal His power to the entire world again. For now, He is content to wait until His kingdom is fully populated before He descends to rule with a rod of iron! He will work miracles that prove His presence. The people of God will continue to prosper while He is squeezing glory from His enemies. People often think they don't have to let you go and serve God. Whenever God gets ready, He will open the door for your release, no matter how many demons are guarding it!

REFLECTION:

April 30

"I have testimony weightier than that of John. For the very work that the Father has given me to finish, and which I am doing, testifies that the Father has sent me" (John 5:36 New International Version).

Jesus lived His life glorifying God. The things He did proved His mission wasn't His own. Do you know anyone else who lived 33 years and never did one selfish thing? God spoke highly of Him even in the Old Testament. There aren't many people God speaks highly of, and certainly none more than His only begotten Son. Jesus had the most important job in the universe. The redemption of mankind wasn't exactly something "anyone" could do. Then, He also volunteered for the job knowing it would cost Him everything. People think that because He is Jesus there was no need for faith. He needed to trust God more than anyone else. Carrying the weight of the world's sin meant He had to believe God would crush His body yet preserve your soul. Then, He had to be resurrected from the dead. Isaac submitted to his own death because he trusted Abraham, and Abraham trusted God.

We need to allow God to shape our perspective concerning Jesus. His humanity was no more human than our humanity. He wasn't walking the earth as some super-human hero. He was a baby, a boy, an adolescent, a young man, then a man. Sounds like a common progression to me.

REFLECTION:

MAY

May 1

"And to know the love of Christ which passeth knowledge, that ye might be filled with all the fullness of God" (Ephesians 3:19 King James Version).

This is a tremendous "wish" that Paul is hoping for the church at Ephesus. How can you possibly know something that exceeds your capacity to know? There was once a commercial for a candy bar that was said to be "indescribably delicious." I'm certainly not comparing a candy bar to God, but Paul is trying to say that you have to know God apart from logic and human comprehension. When it comes to God, you can only EXPERIENCE HIM! Your testimony isn't necessarily your explanation of God as much as it is your encounter with Him. Paul also wanted this beloved church to be filled with the fullness of God.

Jesus had the fullness of the Godhead within Him. Therefore, He had unlimited power, not just potential. Can we have unlimited power? I believe we can walk in the Spirit in such a manner that He can do with us whatever He desires. The fullness of God can only come about as you submit to His authority. You must have a passionate prayer life, intimate time in His word, and regular denying of your own will. When you are truly enjoying the fullness of God, you'll be the last one to know it.

REFLECTION:

May 2

"Teach me to do thy will, For Thou art my God; Let Thy good Spirit lead me on level ground" (Psa ms 143:10 New American Standard).

You serve a God that delights in answering prayer if you serve the God of the Bible. If you're His child, He already has you on His mind. If you're not His child, He still wants to answer your prayer, but it MUST be the sinner's prayer for salvation. David pleads for instruction because he doesn't always see the will of God clearly. We should all want to be led by the Spirit on a smooth path. God sometimes has to put "bumps" on the road to teach us to trust Him. Whatever the case, prayer is ALWAYS in order. Everything that happens in you life is for the will of God to be revealed. Don't worry; He hasn't forgotten you, and He's still just a prayer away.

REFLECTION:

May 3

"But I have received everything in full and have an abundance; I am amply supplied, having received from Epaphroditus what you have sent, a fragrant aroma, an acceptable sacrifice, well-pleasing to God" (Philippians 4:18 New American Standard).

Many Bible readers know what the 19th verse in this chapter says, so I wanted to look at some of the previous verses. Paul was a man that believed if he did the will of God, God would meet his needs. He never asked for anything in his travels even when he reminded the saints of their obligations concerning those chosen to preach the gospel. Things have plummeted dramatically these days. An alarming number of modern preachers are simply creative marketing hustlers! Ask the Lord to direct your decisions when it comes to where you will sew His money. After all, it IS His money.

There are many shepherds who genuinely love God's people, but you don't often get to hear about them. I don't think the ones you see on television have a great financial need like Paul did. It would be wise for you to profit from their ministry and still give where the need exists. There's no law that says you have to give tithes to the radio or television ministry you enjoy. Your support should go to the shepherds, not just the preachers. Who do you call when your children are sick? Who do you call when there's a family emergency? Why call one person when you need prayer and another person when you give an offering? If the person receiving the offering isn't available to minister to you personally, God's money is wasted. Paul is a great example of a shepherd.

REFLECTION:

May 4

"Let our outcasts stay among you. Hide them from our enemies until the terror is past. When oppression and destruction have ceased and enemy raiders have disappeared" (Isaiah 16:4 New Living Translation).

If you are going through a tough time right now, consider yourself an outcast. Now, believe that God is moving on the heart of someone who will welcome you. The Lord is a God of provision, and He wants to soften the heart of a servant who will share with you. When God provides for you, don't forget to do the same for others in the household of faith. Don't close your cupboards to the hungry. Don't hide your faucets from the thirsty. Don't pretend that everything you own is dedicated, and therefore you can't share.

The Bible tells us that if anyone ignores the cries of the needy, they too will cry and none will hear! God is in the business of restoring the outcast. Once you are restored, you understand what is necessary for restoration. Generosity is the order of the kingdom. If we take care of each other, God will take care of enemy raiders. The real tragedy happens when we turn our kindred over to the destroyers. If you can help and you don't help, you have just turned your kindred over to the destroyer. Hunger, thirst, and lack is a reality we live with. We should be doing all we can to eliminate those realities.

REFLECTION:

May 5

"For I am confident of this very thing, that He who began a good work in you will perfect it until the day of Christ Jesus" (Philippians 1:6 New American Standard).

When you accepted Christ, your new life began. When we have children, the responsible thing to do is to raise them the best we can. God is also responsible to raise His children the best He can! Paul had great confidence in God's ability to do this, which is why he thanked God for the Philippians. The seed of the word was planted in you, and it brought forth the spiritual life God our Father intended. You have many stages you must go through on your way to spiritual maturity. We have to cooperate with the will of God if we are to grow strong and wise. Since the work God started is an internal work, shouldn't we be concerned with how external things will affect us internally? God wants to make sure your diet is proper, your rest is regular, and your influences are healthy, too.

Paul expressed confidence for a number of reasons. First, he knew personally that God looks after His own. Second, he witnessed the faithful hand of God in the lives of these believers. It can be difficult for us to comprehend what God is doing. It helps when others tell us what they see God doing in our lives. God's work gives you confidence and develops your own testimony.

REFLECTION:

May 6

"Jesus said to them, 'My food is to do the will of Him who sent Me and to accomplish His work'" (John 4:34 New American Standard).

Jesus not only understood His mission, He also understood the limited time frame He had to fulfill it. I haven't met anyone who was so totally focused on God's calling that it is considered their food! Think about it: your food is something that demands a certain amount of time and attention every day, multiple times a day. When God places a calling on your life, He leaves you the privilege of completing what He started. He completes His work in you while you complete His work on earth. The disciples were concerned that Jesus hadn't eaten, and He wanted to assure them that He was taking care of God's business. The Lord wants to accomplish a number of things while He has you in place representing Him. When you have the satisfaction of knowing your life reflects the will of God, it's even more satisfying than your favorite meal.

REFLECTION:

May 7

"And with them Heman and Jeduthun, and the rest that were chosen, who were expressed by name, to give thanks to the LORD, because his mercy [endureth] forever" (I Chronicles 16:43 King James Version).

Celebrating the wonder of God should be a special event and a special occasion. God often assembled musicians and singers to pave the way for His presence. We should consider praise and worship God's entourage. Because He is grand, He can't help but make a grand entrance. Heman and Jeduthun aren't exactly household names when it comes to characters in the Bible. God mentioned them because they were worth mentioning since their purpose was to help lead the praise processional.

Did you know that YOU were also CHOSEN to help lead a praise processional? You may not be a household name in your church, but if your name is written in heaven, that's the household you should be concerned about. It is important for those who know the goodness of God to express it continually. His mercy endureth: which means it continues uninterrupted. His praise and His adoration should likewise continue uninterrupted. Mercy is a concession that God made in Christ to withhold the punishment you deserved and still deserve.

REFLECTION:

_____

_____

_____

_____

_____

_____

_____

_____

_____

_____

May 8

"In everything we do, we try to show that we are true ministers of God. We patiently endure troubles and hardships and calamities of every kind" (II Corinthians 6:4 New Living Translation).

Did you know that people are watching everything you do? Opinions are formed, and you don't even get to contribute words to those opinions. Paul watched how he handled trials because people will swear you shouldn't hurt like other people hurt. He governed his actions so that the ministry would not be blamed. Can you really prevent someone from "blaming" the ministry or blaming God? I'll leave that answer to you. Paul was very interested in the impression onlookers would form from just watching him. I don't think many of us today are too concerned. After all, you're not perfect. After all, you're trying your best, and they can't see things from your vantage point. We have to be balanced. We certainly shouldn't be paranoid about the viewpoints of others. However, we shouldn't be negligent about it either.

Some people are just impossible to please. Some people will rarely have anything good to say about you. If you're in ministry, ask yourself when was the last time someone expressed appreciation for what you do? Even those who claim to love you will normally forget that it takes a great sacrifice to do the work of the ministry. Be like Paul and David and encourage yourself in the Lord!

REFLECTION:

May 9

"He has walled up my way so that I cannot pass, and He has put darkness on my paths" (Job 19:8 New American Standard).

The book of Job gives us a glimpse into the ways that good and evil interact. Few other books give us a controversial vantage point for what God allows. Who was actually responsible for what happened to Job? Was it God; or was it Satan? I know it was Satan that literally afflicted Job. But I also know it was God that gave him permission to do it. The human mind can't comprehend the benefit of affliction. It almost sounds morbid to use the words "benefit" and "affliction" in the same sentence. Job's perspective seems to focus only on God. Although Job knew evil existed (he offered sacrifices), he never blamed Satan for his condition. He appealed to the Lord for relief and understanding, yet it never came. He appealed to his friends for compassion, yet it never came. Why would a loving God "do" such a thing? Did He do it to show Satan how weak he actually is? Did He want to prove that inner goodness is greater than any evil circumstance? I don't know why He did it. And, no offense, but you don't know either! He did it because He decided it was a necessary ingredient to conform Job to His image. That is also why you're dealing with your afflictions, too. God has you closed in, and He has temporarily turned out the lights.

REFLECTION:

May 10

"Just think of Him Who endured from sinners such grievous opposition and bitter hostility against Himself [reckon up and consider it all in comparison with your trials], so that you may not grow weary or exhausted, losing heart and relaxing and fainting in your minds" (Hebrews 12:3 Amplified Bible).

When things get really rough and difficult to handle, most normal people tend to wonder why they have it so bad. We don't think we deserve it, and we certainly don't think it is justice for some forgotten deed. The book of Hebrews doesn't give us much time to think about ourselves. We live in a country that wastes enough to take care of the entire world. While we soak in our little pity party, the Lord is trying to motivate us. Even if you can think of someone who suffered like Jesus did, you can't prove they were innocent while suffering.

All of us are guilty at some point, even if we are moral and outstanding citizens. Compare your trials to the trials of Christ and see how long you feel sorry for yourself. Yes, our troubles are real, so were His. Yes, our pain is real, so was His. The reason why He is the most qualified helper is because He knows EXACTLY what it feels like. The point of this passage is to encourage you so that you won't give up. When you remember how much worse it was for Him, you can look ahead and wait for brighter days. If He could endure His course for you, why can't you endure yours for Him?

REFLECTION:

139

May 11

"Therefore, as God's chosen people, holy and dearly loved, clothe yourselves with compassion, kindness, humility, gentleness and patience" (Colossians 3:12 New International Version).

This verse starts with the word therefore because of what Jesus did in the previous verses. Our behavior changed towards one another because of His behavior toward us. He became what He needed from Him. Can we become what others need from us? This verse also has a combination of the fruit of the Spirit and the armor of God. When we are instructed to "put on" anything, we need to make a choice. You didn't have a choice until God put power within reach. Christ removed the divisions that man erected. There is no Jew or Gentile, bond or free, and even male or female. Does that mean these distinctions don't exist anymore? No, they still exist. However, as far as God is concerned, these distinctions don't determine His acceptance of us.

We should now see each other the way God sees. The virtues mentioned above can only prevail when you look through the eyes of Christ. Compassion understands weakness without excusing it. Kindness ministers to weakness without justifying it. Humility relates to weakness without defending it. Gentleness removes weakness without rejecting it. Patience outlasts weakness without regretting it.

REFLECTION:

May 12

"Therefore, Jesus lifting up His eyes, and seeing that a large crowd was coming to Him, said to Philip, 'Where are we to buy bread, so that these may eat?'" (John 6:5 New American Standard).

If you look back over your life, there have been many times where Jesus tested you. He is always with you, and He wants you to see things through His eyes. He knew exactly what He was going to do. However, you don't know exactly what He is going to do. The disciples wouldn't normally have carried the burden of feeding a multitude.

If you're going to be "fishers" of men, you also have to be concerned with being "feeders" of men. Philip knew they were faced with a problem beyond normal human solution. Isn't it interesting that Philip didn't ask Jesus where the money would come from? Jesus will walk you right into an issue that you can't handle without Him. Sometimes we act like He can't handle it either. If you had the money, where would you get the bread? The question assumes the power but asks about the resources. The answer: the Bread of Life has the power, knows the resource, and is the food!

REFLECTION:

May 13

"There is no fear in love. But perfect love drives out fear, because fear has to do with punishment. The one who fears is not made perfect in love" (I John 4:18 New International Version).

I happen to believe there is a difference between fear and being afraid. To me, and this is certainly debatable, to be afraid happens when something catches you unaware. Fear is often a result of thought patterns concerning something or someone. How does perfect love drive out fear? The only perfect love is the love of God. His love drives out fear because we know He isn't handling us according to our understanding. We still must RECEIVE this love in order for it to drive out any fear. The expected punishment that comes from fear is real because we're really guilty!

The love of God, when received, brings the relief of forgiveness. The relief of forgiveness provides the motivation for service, the foundation for courage, and the platform for praise. John was the most qualified one to speak concerning love. He leaned on the chest of Jesus at dinner time. He gave himself to understand the love of God through the actions of God. I don't believe God loved him more than the other disciples. I also don't believe he loved God more than the other disciples. I just happen to believe he opened himself more to understand the love of God.

REFLECTION:

May 14

"But we ought always to give thanks to God for you, brothers beloved by the Lord, because God chose you as the first fruits to be saved, through sanctification by the Spirit and belief in the truth" (II Thessalonians 2:13 English Standard Version).

How many other people are thankful that God chose you? Does anyone regularly tell you how thankful they are that you are beloved of the Lord? I want to make it my business to accept this verse as a personal challenge to remember God's value in others when I'm praying for them. I also want to tell them how good it is that they were chosen. It should make your day to know that YOU are a choice of God to partake of the first fruits of salvation. I know it is two thousand years later, but in God's mind, it all happens right now.

Paul was not only willing but eager to praise God for the fruit of the gospel. Paul established the church, but laborers had to keep the work fruitful. It is a blessing to see something you planted get the necessary nourishment to grow. These people were a garden that Paul was able to see growing. When God has chosen you, the evidence comes forth. The Spirit of God works in you to produce the manifestation of His presence. Without God, you wouldn't have had the intelligence to recognize the truth, accept the truth, believe the truth, or apply the truth.

REFLECTION:

May 15

"Pray in the Spirit at all times and on every occasion. Stay alert and be persistent in your prayers for all believers everywhere" (Ephesians 6:18 New Living Translation).

It appears God's people have become so accustomed to His goodness that prayer has diminished to something we do on special occasions. We have prayer meetings once in a while. We have church meetings constantly. We have fasts and consecrations once in a while. We have feasts and conversations constantly. I would like to discover just how many times Paul mentioned prayer in his letters to various churches. I'm sure he didn't mention it as often as he thought of it; but he mentioned it lots of times.

What does it mean to pray in the Spirit? I believe it means to pray with the direction of the Holy Spirit. I believe it means to pray under the influence of the Holy Spirit. Finally, I believe it means to pray while submitted to the Holy Spirit. When you read certain passages, it appears as though God wants us praying constantly. We assume that you can't constantly be praying. We should be aware of the need for prayer, the power in prayer, and the victory by prayer, and the persistence through prayer. In other words, PRAY!

REFLECTION:

_____

_____

_____

_____

_____

_____

_____

_____

_____

May 16

"Trust in the LORD with all your heart, and do not lean on your own understanding" (Proverbs 3:5 New American Standard).

I know this is a favorite and widely known verse among the people of God. It is often connected with verse six, which tells us to acknowledge God in every way so our path can be directed by Him. I deliberately chose to talk about this verse without verse six for a change. Trust is a big problem with the people of God. If we have trouble trusting God, we must ask ourselves how well we know Him. Your trust in any relationship is based on dependability, track record, and familiarity. You only trust those you know really well.

Trusting God with all your heart encompasses an unwavering response, even when it looks strange. Didn't it seem strange for God to tell Abraham to sacrifice Isaac? Yet, Abraham decided that God must be planning something that includes fulfilling His promise, even if it means immediate resurrection. We can't lean on our own "understanding." Your understanding is also defined as: "what you think God will do." You can't even lean on your own interpretation of His word. Can God do something that you think is a contradiction of His word? If He does, then I guess you had the wrong "understanding." Do what He says, not what you thought He said.

REFLECTION:

_____

_____

_____

_____

_____

_____

_____

_____

_____

May 17

"But in all these things we overwhelmingly conquer through Him who loved us" (Romans 8:37 New American Standard).

When was the last time you considered the love of Christ an empowering factor? We mostly see love as something just to be enjoyed. But the love of Christ is also something to be employed! To be more than a conqueror means we have a surpassing victory, a prevailing victory, an encompassing victory. When the love of Christ is behind you, everything in front of you is defeated. As you examine your own life, "all these things" means whatever you're going through.

Paul could write these words because he knew that nothing created or even uncreated could separate us from the love of Christ. Job has poetically revealed to us that man born of a woman is of a few days and full of trouble. The psalmist has also poetically revealed to us that many are the afflictions of the righteous, but the Lord delivers us out of them all. Yes, we live our lives torn between the two extremes of valleys and mountains. However, when the time comes for surpassing, when the time comes for prevailing, when the time comes for encompassing, you will be standing strong once and for all!

REFLECTION:

May 18

"And the Lord shall deliver me from every evil work and will preserve me unto his heavenly kingdom: to whom be glory forever and ever. Amen" (II Timothy 4:18 King James Version).

The word deliver has two very interesting meanings. One meaning is to "set free." The other is "to take to an intended recipient." You HAVE been successfully set free from every evil work. There will be bad intentions, but no bad outcomes. All that is meant for evil, God intends for your good. Once again, there is no such thing as a Christian "victim." Everything that happens to you will still serve as an ingredient for God's plan in your destiny! God's declaration toward you also includes a destination. You are headed somewhere beyond your imagination. All of heaven is expecting you. Your preservation is for your reservation! You are in Christ, and Christ is in God. There are no missing parts in the body of Christ. There are no unnecessary parts in the body of Christ. The Father, Son, and Holy Spirit have all joined forces to make sure nothing cancels His travel plan for you.

REFLECTION:

May 19

"It was not by their sword that they won the land, nor did their arm bring them victory; it was your right hand, your arm, and the light of your face, for you loved them" (Psalms 44:3 New International Version)

We should make the most of our opportunities to get preparation. We should always get in position for the most influence. However, your work isn't what guarantees victory. Sometimes success can bring contempt. People tend to think it was their own abilities and connections that win battles. When the people of God forget to acknowledge God, defeat is waiting for you around the corner. Gather the troops, load the weapons, plan the battle, then say your prayers.

The right hand and the right arm of God are symbolic of strength, power, and authority. The light of God's face is symbolic of direction and favor. Because God loves you, the benefits are tremendous. After you have done everything you can do to get ready, take your hands off the steering wheel. There's lots of territory to be gained. The ranks of God need to advance and begin the takeover. If God didn't intend for you to takeover, why would He arm you with a sword? The psalmist understood that God had plans to exalt His people, and at the same time, diminish and vanquish His foes.

REFLECTION:

May 20

"He said to him, 'If they do not hear Moses and the prophets, neither will they be convinced if someone should rise from the dead'" (Luke 16:31 Revised Standard Version).

This conversation was held in the afterlife. These words were spoken by Abraham to the rich man that treated Lazarus poorly during his lifetime. The man wanted Abraham to send Lazarus first to dip his finger in water and cool his tongue because of the tormenting flames. Then, he wanted Lazarus to warn his brothers not to come to his eternal fate. Isn't it interesting that if the servants of God don't convince you, nothing will? Things really haven't changed much.

Anyone unwilling to hear Moses and the prophets today won't believe in Jesus either, even though He rose from the dead. This text also proves that people are aware of what happens on earth after they die. Abraham explained how this man was comforted, and Lazarus was tormented. Now, the roles are reversed permanently. Moses and the prophets simply pointed to faith in Jesus Christ. We have a better chance of convincing people to believe while we're here. Your testimony confirms the truth contained in the words of Moses and the prophets. Their words and yours magnify Jesus.

REFLECTION:

May 21

"They promise them freedom, but they themselves are slaves of corruption. For whatever overcomes a person, to that he is enslaved" (II Peter 2:19 English Standard Version).

Everyone functioning in an influential position wasn't called by God to fulfill that position. Many ascended to leadership in order to take advantage of open doors and open hearts. The Bible is a book of liberty, despite man's attempts to legalize and legislate their own opinions. The liberty the Bible teaches is the freedom to serve God and the freedom to say no to your flesh. Before your relationship with Christ, you didn't have the fortitude to overpower your desires.

Peter tells this group of believers that many of the very ones preaching freedom are slaves to the corruption of their carnal nature. Everyone has a carnal nature no matter how long you have been saved. The goal is to make that carnal nature submit to the will of God for your life. It seems strange that your worst enemy is within. If we are habitually overcome by the demands of the old nature, we have become slaves again. Unfortunately, many believers are sitting in prisons that Jesus already unlocked.

REFLECTION:

May 22

"That is why we never give up. Though our bodies are dying, our spirits are being renewed every day" (II Corinthians 4:16 New Living Translation).

Paul was an unbelievable man of faith. He reckoned his own life pointless unless it rendered glory to God. He was content to have his life poured out if it meant others could be filled through his emptiness. All of us have had occasions where we just wanted to "pack it in." One reason we never give up is that everything contributes to a positive end. We would never subscribe to many of the things we go through, but it will be a necessary component in the molding process. We can't forget that God has an image in mind for us. He will file us, sand us, carve us, squeeze us, wash us, iron us, chisel us, and break us until we conform to that image.

He won't override our will, but He certainly knows how to superimpose His design on us. Romans 9:19 asks an intriguing question, "For who has resisted his will?" I don't want to debate that with any of you. Our job is to never give up because we know that God is accomplishing something great through every event of our lives. The perishing of the body doesn't infect the spirit.

REFLECTION:

May 23

"And coming up at that very hour she began to give thanks to God and to speak of him to all who were waiting for the redemption of Jerusalem" (Luke 2:38 English Standard Version).

These are the words of the prophetess Anna. We don't normally hear about her in the Christmas story, but she is a major player, too. Why else would God have her enter the temple at the time Jesus was being presented? Anna knew she was beholding the face of mankind's only hope. Don't you see that Anna was the first evangelist? Anna knew when Jesus was still a baby that He was the answer to all who were waiting. God remembered the promise made to His people. God remembers what He promised you, too. Anna offered thanks to God for the Offering that came from God.

What are you waiting for? Do you believe that God has already answered your hopes with this same Jesus? Nothing is more valuable than your eternal redemption. Yet, God has solved every other problem you could have by solving your biggest problem. Mankind's biggest problem was where he would spend eternity. Anna helped fashion the gospel message even before Jesus died. Now, we can give thanks to God and speak about Him to those who are waiting.

REFLECTION:

May 24

"And indeed if they had been thinking that country from which they went out, they would have had opportunity to return" (Hebrews 11:15 New American Standard).

When Hebrews defines faith as the substance of things hoped for and the evidence of things unseen, it causes us to look deeper into what God is actually doing. Faith not only trusts God regardless of current events, but faith looks to a promising future. If you regard yesterday as "the good ol' days," and you're hesitant about moving forward, you are NOT walking by faith. When you walk with God, your focus must remain on where He is leading you. Deliverance is permanent when your focus is forward.

The heroes of the faith that God wants to highlight in this chapter knew their country wasn't the physical one. Your mind greatly influences your direction. God leads us out, but it's up to us to close the mental doors behind us. Do you think your past is better than your future? If so, I would challenge you to think again. Your current dilemma has nothing to do with your future deliverance. Keep looking for the better things; keep expecting a brighter day. Keep looking up.

REFLECTION:

May 25

"Even before he made the world, God loved us and chose us in Christ to be holy and without fault in his eyes" (Ephesians 1:4 New Living Translation).

My question for you today is: do you know who you are? You were the biggest part of God's decision-making process. He made the world after He thought about you because He needed an environment perfectly suited for you. He had the foresight to know what you like the most. He had the compassion to provide the right temperature, the right moisture balance, the right sun exposure, and the right shadows and shades. He provided the food that makes your mouth water. Best of all, He provided Himself.

Now, the thing that occupies the mind of God is returning you to that original intent. In fact, the outcome will be even better than the outset. The first environment was a perfect match; the last environment will be a better match. You were chosen. Being holy and without fault wasn't something you accomplished. What you have is what He afforded you. As sinful as we are, He has declared us without fault. The key is that He sees us in Christ. He saw us in Adam as king of the earth. He sees us in Christ as King of the heavens and the earth.

REFLECTION:

May 26

"For the kingdom of God does not consist in talk but in power" (I Corinthians 4:20 English Standard Version).

Paul was fed up with "hearing" about those who could talk a good game. Even now, we are inundated with radio, television and even internet personalities that have a lot to say. When you're deciding who to support, who to promote, and where to attend, do you know anything about the power behind their words? Yes, it is certainly important that a person be a good communicator. But do you stop there? Being able to encourage, challenge, and motivate God's people comes along with the gift. The Holy Spirit brings His power along with His gifts. He also bears fruit along with His gifts and His power. You can usually tell quite a bit about a leader by observing their followers.

A good leader is committed to EMPOWERING followers. God equips His leaders with the ability to affect change. Jesus poured Himself into a group of followers. When He finished with them, they would change the world and influence generations. The kingdom of God must be distinct from all other kingdoms. The kingdom of God should reflect the power of the King. Jesus changed everything: now it's our turn!

REFLECTION:

May 27

"We are writing these things so that you may fully share our joy" (I John 1:4 New Living Translation).

John knew what a special relationship he had with Jesus Christ. Whenever anyone gets close to God, they want everyone to share and know that same joy. Many of us don't have that same passion anymore. John was so passionate; he wrote to those he couldn't talk to in person. These words aren't for any certain group. John felt his children were those who received the message he preached. So, no matter where this letter lands, it will speak to someone. If an unbeliever comes to faith in Christ because of what you share, your joy will most certainly increase.

I wonder how many of us care what God considers full joy? We spend our lives fighting over positions and possessions that will never bring full joy. This is the kind of joy that must be shared in order to be full! If we had enough money for everyone in the world to be rich, we would be giving it away freely. We have enough gospel for everyone in the world to be spiritually rich without taking away from our riches. So, why aren't we giving this away like money?

REFLECTION:

May 28

"This is evidence of the righteous judgment of God, that you may be considered worthy of the kingdom of God, for which you are also suffering" (II Thessalonians 1:5 English Standard Version).

This church endured much affliction for their testimony of Jesus Christ. Paul is commending them because they endured the suffering with patience. We can't stand to suffer, let alone suffer with patience. God gives the grace to endure hardships while maintaining a good countenance towards God. I happen to believe the corporate faith of the church will be tested in varying degrees. Individuals will certainly be tested. I also think congregations will be tested and denominations too. Those who never had to worry about finances will begin to see their coffers shrinking. For God to consider us worthy, He has to see how well we handle adversity. Whoever can't handle prosperity can't handle adversity either.

True riches are spiritual ones. You don't have to be a Christian a long time for God to consider you worthy of His kingdom benefits. God is righteous in all of His dealings, no matter what we think of Him. Suffering has its place in the faith, and it too will accomplish the ultimate will of God for all of us.

REFLECTION:

May 29

"He moved away from there and dug another well, and they did not quarrel over it; so he named it Rehoboth, for he said, 'At last the LORD has made room for us, and we will be fruitful in the land'" (Genesis 26:22 New American Standard).

It is quite interesting that I only recall the Bible mentioning Isaac as a patriarch who was involved in digging wells. Isaac was the first child of the promise, yet he went on an expedition to discover fresh sources of provision in his personal pursuit of God. Although we are spiritual children of Abraham through Isaac, we should "dig," working with our hands in order to find the area of expertise that God can make fruitful. The name Rehoboth means "wide places" or "streets."

When God decides to bless the works of your hands, He opens avenues of revenue and makes it possible for you to pave the way for others. We should never do anything with purely selfish motives. The glory of God will always include others who will be improved by His hand upon you. When Proverbs tells you that your gift makes room for you, it is better translated that your gift opens doors for you as the giver. I'm sure many were blessed greatly by Isaac's sacrifice. When you give your gift(s) freely, God can function as your employer since He gave you the idea anyway. God takes outstanding care of His servants. His benefits continue to yield long after you stop working.

REFLECTION:

158

May 30

"So, you also must consider yourselves dead to sin and alive to God in Christ Jesus" (Romans 6:11 English Standard Version).

What perspective should we have on the reality of sin in our lives? I know some believers who have actually convinced themselves they don't sin. When this verse tells us to consider ourselves dead to sin, it means that sin shouldn't have a dominating position over us. This is the main reason that all addictions are sinful. Christ died so that we should never have to say, "I can't help it."

The only thing that keeps us bound to addictions is fear and temporary pleasure. We are all servants of something; no one is independent of servitude. You will either satisfy God, satisfy Satan, or satisfy self. The goal in being a follower of Christ is that we satisfy God, especially in those areas where we have satisfied ourselves. We will sin until we go to heaven, but it should be unintentional. How much power does sin really have until we submit to it?

REFLECTION:

May 31

"So then, brothers, stand firm and hold to the teachings we passed on to you, whether by word of mouth or by letter" (II Thessalonians 2:15 New International Version).

The word of God is to be esteemed whether it is written or spoken. Sometimes, we are slow to respond to the word if we don't like the preacher or writer. We will be held accountable for the word we have been given. You don't have to like the glass to drink the water! God may purposely send you a word through someone you don't respect or admire. If the person is speaking the truth, it's as though the Lord Himself is speaking. Thank God that He cares enough about you to send a rescue word in season. The same word you ignore today might be the word you will need tomorrow.

REFLECTION:

_____

_____

_____

_____

_____

_____

_____

_____

_____

_____

_____

_____

_____

_____

JUNE

June 1

"You search the Scriptures because you think that in them you have eternal life, and it is they that bear witness about me" (John 5:39 English Standard Version).

It is always a good idea to search and investigate the scriptures. However, when you search through the word of God, you should not be searching for facts, figures, or feelings. When you come away from the word of God, you should feel like the words are trying to introduce you to a PERSON. If you already know the person, you should feel the need to know the person a little better every time you open the Bible.

One of the biggest tragedies in the Bible is that the ones with their noses in the word the most didn't understand what the words were trying to teach. Jesus made it abundantly clear that He is the one the Scriptures tried to reveal. Every direct descendant of Abraham was taught to expect the Messiah. Throughout each generation, the expectation was kept fresh and real. Even today, some are still awaiting his arrival, even though He has already come, died, and rose again. You can't read the Bible hoping it will show you a god you want to see. It will show you the God of the universe and prepare you to meet Him.

REFLECTION:

_____

_____

_____

_____

_____

_____

_____

_____

_____

_____

June 2

"For God saved us and cal ed us to live a holy life. He did this, not because we deserved it, but because t at was his plan from before the beginning of time—to show us his grace through Jesus Christ" (II Timothy 1:9 New Living Translation).

God has done many incredible things for us. All of His deeds should compel us to respond in ways that honor Him. God saved us. That should be enough for us to bow before Him, if He never did another thing. But He also called us with a holy calling. What does that mean? It means many things, but primarily it means that we should be careful to represent His nature by our lifestyle. People will never see God. Since they will never see God, the ones chosen to represent Him should show an accurate depiction of His character.

God invested in us by His own choosing. He didn't look at our credentials and decide to pick the best of options. He just set His love upon us. The proof is that He did it before He did anything else. Planning takes into account contingency plans. God knew we would fall, yet He chose us anyway. Grace is best served on the platter of forgiveness. It takes great love to draft a plan that succeeds n perfection, despite our continual failures.

REFLECTION:

June 3

"But we have this treasure in earthen vessels, that the excellency of the power may be of God and not of us" (II Corinthians 4:7 King James Version).

I LOVE this verse. Here's a reasonable question to ask: "Why would God store the priceless inside the worthless?" The reasonable answer is found in the second half of the verse. God is glorified and greatly honored when an unlikely person is successful. The tragedy is that some of us have forgotten that we're just ordinary clay pots who house divine treasure. I once wondered why this verse starts with the conjunction "but." Then I looked at the previous verses and realized that it is a beautiful comparison to what God did in His creative acts.

God intervened in darkness and said, "Let there be light." That's really what He did when He saved us. He intervened into the sinful darkness of our lives and spoke the light of His gospel into us. Therefore, any good thing we can accomplish is due to the presence of the light in us. Don't fall for the new age philosophy that tries to convince you that light is automatically in you. If you don't have a relationship with God through Christ, you're still in the dark.

REFLECTION:

June 4

"For the LORD God is a sun and shield; the LORD gives grace and glory; No good thing does He withhold from those who walk uprightly" (Psalms 84:11 New American Standard).

I love this verse because it clarifies the position God takes with His people. It also clarifies His determination to bless you. God is a sun and shield. The word uses analogies to help us relate to God's influential participation. The sun gives light, warmth, and signifies a new day filled with new opportunities. A shield protects; a shield also hides. Sometimes God prevents your enemies from even locating you. Even if they find you, they can't penetrate His protective covering. God gives grace and glory. Some translations use the words favor and honor.

There are times when God will establish you based on what He knows about you. He puts His reputation on the line until you can build one for yourself. I really get excited just knowing that He won't keep anything from me that will benefit my journey. When I make my decisions with Him in mind, He makes sure that I prosper in my dealings. The psalmist knew the goodness of the Lord in every circumstance. We will also find Him to be faithful in every situation.

REFLECTION:

June 5

"For by one Spirit we were all baptized into one body, whether Jews or Greeks, whether slaves or free, and we were all made to drink of one Spirit" (I Corinthians 12:13 New American Standard).

The fourth chapter of Ephesians tells us a little bit about the unity of the Spirit. The entire Bible tells us about the unity within the entire Godhead. Since we have been baptized by the Spirit into the body of Christ, we must exhibit the fruit of unity, so we don't confuse unbelievers.

God treats us all with dignity regardless of our heritage, our ethnicity, our gender, or our social status. Somehow, we have managed to blur those lines. We should be careful to honor the Spirit in every person God receives. It doesn't promote the message of the Kingdom when we diminish someone for ANY reason. Even if the person is struggling, our responsibility is to restore them to fruitful productivity. Yes, we are our brother's keeper, whether we like it or not, whether we feel like it or not. Since we want to reflect the character of God, it is vitally important that we show great unity.

REFLECTION:

June 6

"Out of the same mouth come praise and cursing. My brothers, this should not be" (James 3:10 New International Version).

James has always been a straight shooter as it relates to practical demonstrations of godliness. In chapter one, he told us that pure and undefiled religion is validated when you visit the widows and the fatherless. In chapter two, he told us to give what is needed instead of just encouraging people to depart and be warmed and filled. Now, in chapter three, he tells us not to be two-mouthed. I sort of made that term up. It is similar to being two-faced. We are commended and commanded to praise God. If anyone knows how much God is worthy of praise, it should be those of us who are His beneficiaries. However, the same fountain that delivers the fresh water of praise to God, also delivers the bitter waters towards the image of God. Therefore, James is revealing the will of God in that we should be consistent.

Would you release those bitter waters when you're communing with God? I certainly hope not! Man is God's crowning achievement and His image on earth. He expects us to refresh each other like we refresh Him.

REFLECTION:

June 7

"Therefore, prepare your minds for action, and being sober-minded, set your hope fully on the grace to be given you when Jesus Christ is revealed" (1 Peter 1:13 New International Version).

One reason we must prepare our minds for action is because God may be using our lives as a sacrifice to benefit someone else. Think about it, the fathers of the faith didn't receive the promise of the Messiah in their lifetime. God has the right to do what He wants with His vessels. He may use some of us as ordinary everyday drinking glasses and others as fine china. Now, the fine china also endures much more testing to be prepared for special occasions. Your mind needs to be ready to accept whatever God has determined for you. Then, after you accept it, embrace it. You can't be prepared for action if you despise His intents for you!

The great news is that when you look at the end of the road, grace is waiting for you at the revelation of Jesus Christ. Let's face it, you might not understand what God is doing until you look into the eyes of Jesus. At that moment, all of your questions will be answered without asking them. You will know everything you need to know and understand everything you need to understand. Until then, set your hope there, and just trust Him.

REFLECTION:

June 8

"You know that everyone in the province of Asia has deserted me, including Phygelus and Hermogenes" (II Timothy 1:15 New International Version).

Every once in a while, you see the vulnerable side of Paul shine through. Anyone serving God wants to be accepted, especially by those you have given a great deal of t me for spiritual growth. Sometimes you will hear Paul say something that bothers him. Then, in the next sentence, he will encourage himself in what God is doing in him. It is one thing for an enemy to resist you, but when a comrade deserts you, it pierces the heart. It must have been especially hurtfu since he used the word "including" in his description.

If you haven't experienced it yet, serving God can cost you friends, business opportunities, and even spouses. We have been told to count the cost associated with saying yes to God. If there is someone or something standing in the way, He wants to know if He can trust you with His plans. It takes a special person to get inside information. You must be a trusted servant to get classified clearance! At least Paul knew he could count on Timothy. God will always give you at least one confidante.

REFLECTION:

June 9

"If anyone considers himself religious and yet does not keep a tight rein on his tongue, he deceives himself and his religion is worthless" (James 1:26 New International Version).

Most of us assume this verse is simply condemning profanity. Don't you know that you can be the worst communicator in the world without any bad language? Consider this: sarcasm and cynicism can enrage a listener faster than anything else. Hollering at another person because you're in a bad mood will shut down any chance of reconciliation. Keeping a tight rein on your tongue has more to do with how you say things than what you actually say. Your emotions carry your words in ways that speak volumes about your intent, your personality, and your priorities. I have taught for years that everything in your mind should not come out of your mouth.

Take the time to think about your words and your emotions because you can't really take back words. All you can do is follow them up with different ones and ask for forgiveness. James believes your communication skills, or lack thereof, will tell what you think of God. He says if you have no control over your own tongue, it translates to God having no ownership over your spirit.

REFLECTION:

June 10

"At the same time, it is a new commandment that I am writing to you, which is true in him and in you, because the darkness is passing away, and the true light is already shining" (I John 2:8 English Standard Version).

John told us that if we claim to abide in Jesus, we should walk in the same manner He walked. Jesus didn't have to deal with darkness in His own character, but He had to navigate through a dark world. He demonstrated to us how it is possible to be in the world without being of the world. Since God has called us out of darkness, we must agree that fellowship without darkness is a deliberate choice. Chances are good that you are more willing to accept your own darkness than the darkness of others. When John shares commandments, he is actually revealing the power available to us as believers. You don't have to be pushed around by your flesh, the world, or even the devil.

The darkness of slavery is passing away through the process of sanctification. The light of liberty strengthens you more and more each day. Walking in the light that is already shining helps us draw closer to the source of that light. It feels good to know that God puts His truth in us and puts opportunities for growth in front of us.

REFLECTION:

June 11

"When I am with those who are weak, I share their weakness, for I want to bring the weak to Christ. Yes, I try to find common ground with everyone, doing everything I can to save some" (I Corinthians 9:22 New Living Translation).

I find it very appalling when a Christian thinks they're better than anyone else. We are called to recognize the grace of God in every situation, especially our own. We can act arrogant and superior, even among other believers. The unbelievers won't be drawn to us when we can't even peacefully coexist within the family of God. If you're going to make Jesus attractive to an unbeliever, you must be able to relate to them. Paul is simply saying that he found common ground in order to share the gospel message with anyone. He isn't saying that he became the same kind of person as them, but he put himself in their shoes.

Jesus humbled Himself in order to relate to us, and He requires us to humble ourselves in order to relate to others. Common ground is necessary because Christ died for all mankind. Don't forget where God found you. Don't forget how messed up you were when He decided to clean you up and transform you into the person you are right now, and don't forget that you still haven't become who He wants you to be. You're a work in progress.

REFLECTION:

June 12

"How lonely sits the city that was full of people! She has become like a widow who was once great among the nations! The princess among the provinces Has become a slave" (Lamentations 1:1 New American Standard).

Although this verse talks about Jerusalem, the principle can apply to individuals, churches, cities, and nations. As much as I hate to say it, we live in a nation that God has blessed so abundantly, we now act as though He must continue to bless us. The only thing most of us seem content to do is voice discontent. When anyone disagrees, our solution is to crucify them. We have become adept at masking personal agendas under the cloak of righteousness. This country is only a moment away from chastening. We ask God to have His way, and then when He has His way, we refuse to accept the outcome as His way!

Jeremiah lamented for God's people and God's city. When will we wake up and understand that God makes His moves based on the response of His people and not the reactions of the wicked. This verse has three sentences, and each one ends with an exclamation point. God is trying to get someone's attention. How long will people and groups assume He's always talking to everyone else except them?

REFLECTION:

June 13

"For I testify about them that they have a zeal for God, but not in accordance with knowledge" (Romans 10:2 New American Standard).

As you can clearly see, sincerity alone doesn't get the job done. As someone adequately said ages ago, "You can be sincere, and be sincerely wrong!" Paul had a tremendous burden for all lost souls but especially for those who were God's chosen people. Even God's chosen people still have to choose Him. The exaltation of Jesus Christ is something very difficult for the descendants of Israel to accept. Just think how you would feel if everything you have ever believed for generations was being "amended?" The Jews were required to be a very dedicated and faithful people.

The task of anyone carrying the gospel message is to be patient and understanding. There are many groups with an abundance of zeal. We have an abundance of knowledge because of the Holy Spirit. If we can put the best of both worlds together, there would be countless people responding properly to the call for salvation. Paul had great zeal, and God imparted great knowledge, too. We should commit to increasing zeal in order to share our knowledge with more lost souls.

REFLECTION:

June 14

"Therefore, do not throw away your confidence, which has a great reward" (Hebrews 10:35 New American Standard).

We have numerous reasons to hold on until the end of this race. For one thing, God has never broken a promise. There are many other servants of the Lord left on record that thought doom was imminent. Your confidence in the power of God is the vehicle that will carry you through every obstacle you face. The book of Hebrews was written to remind us of the superiority of Jesus. Kingdom promises are better, and they are enduring.

Israel walked in covenant with God. The church walks in covenant with Jesus. There is great reward in store when the Father turns universal authority over to the Son. Actually, it has already been given to Jesus, but there is a day coming when it will be consummated. Esau sold his birthright for a bowl of stew. Judas sold his inheritance for 30 pieces of silver. What is it you have confidence in? All of us have placed our allegiance somewhere. You have access to the only power that cannot be effectively resisted. We can't comprehend what it means to have unlimited power. It isn't possible to understand what is infinite. Do you know anyone else that can simply speak and cause everything to move by one word?

REFLECTION:

June 15

"So, this is the situation: Most of the people of Israel have not found the favor of God they are looking for so earnestly. A few have--the ones God has chosen--but the hearts of the rest were hardened" (Romans 11:7 New Living Translation).

The book of Romans is one of the most profound, doctrinal, and practical books in the entire word of God. Paul does a masterful job explaining (by revelation) what God was really up to in choosing a people for His name. Although the Jews were His chosen nation, not all of them will embrace Jesus as their Messiah. God chose them, but most of them didn't choose Him. Even today, God so loved the world that He gave Jesus, but most of the world won't choose Him either! A common denominator is that God will accomplish His will through a remnant.

So many have studied the scriptures, yet they missed who the scriptures tried to reveal. Have you ever looked for something, looked right over it, and then continued to look for it? God so orchestrated salvation that those who thought they were entitled to it missed it because they didn't value it. Those who weren't selected first hungered for it and found it because they valued it. Then, those who were offered it first got jealous of those who valued it and found it. God truly loves the entire world.

REFLECTION:

June 16

"He thought it was better to suffer for the sake of Christ than to own the treasures of Egypt, for he was looking ahead to his great reward" (Hebrews 11:26 New Living Translation).

Ouch! This verse should pierce every sellout with a lightning bolt of conviction. How many times have you heard someone say that the world was a much better option because the church doesn't pay well? How many other situations do you know of where a secular artist left the church for the glitz and glam of Hollywood or Vegas? Well, I'm not really suggesting that everyone who needs to choose should choose poverty.

Sometimes the church can be overbearing and think you should forsake the best "package" available. I guess the difference is whether or not you sense the call of God to do what you do. If you're just showcasing your talents, then go get paid. If you're responding to a burden, then you must understand that God will take care of you. God has great riches in store for anyone that invests in Him. Suffering for the sake of Christ doesn't always mean abject poverty. Moses wasn't poor by any stretch of the imagination. His suffering was the rejection of being identified with God. Most of us understand that choosing God makes you a target for His enemies. Make sure you fulfill your calling: God won't accept any excuses from you if He gave you His burden.

REFLECTION:

June 17

"And our hope for you is firmly grounded, knowing that as you are sharers of our sufferings, so also are you sharers of our comfort" (II Corinthians 1:7 New American Standard).

If you are going to be used by God in any sort of leadership capacity, you must exhibit great patience. The book of James tells us that patience results when your faith is tried. Even after patience is produced, you must let it work in you and come to maturity. In spite of the issues present at the church in Corinth, Paul showed great patience with them. Rebuke is a natural element of mentoring. God uses suffering to stretch your faith. If you remain steadfast when He stretches you, He won't have to worry about you when things get tough.

Paul knew he could be confident in the Corinthian church once they handled hardships properly and once they responded well to correction. When God can trust you, it is only a matter of time until He sends you to do greater works. He doesn't test you because He needs to find out about you. He tests you because YOU need to find out about you! The word consolation in this verse means: partner, companion, or sharer. God makes sure you get the benefits of the job and not just the work associated with the job.

REFLECTION:

June 18

"We have confidence in the Lord concerning you, that you are doing and will continue to do what we command" (II Thessalonians 3:4 New American Standard).

It warms the heart of a spiritual leader when he can be confident that you follow the Lord. The things Paul commanded are things from the heart of God. Do you submit to your spiritual leaders in a way that helps them sleep at night? Or do you grieve them in a way that keeps them awake at night? When you do the will of God, it is a blessing to everyone in the local church, your family, and the body of Christ. God manifests His pleasure in you and makes your work fruitful.

Just like it is difficult to find good help in the secular realm, it is difficult to find good help in the spiritual realm. The days of "donating" your gift until God gives the increase are practically gone. Most people want to be paid from the start. Don't get me wrong; I believe the laborer is worthy of his wages, but who gets paid before they have done work? The continuation of doing good is what makes the long-term difference. Faithfulness is the accumulation of regular behavior that creates an expectation. When someone observes you long enough to have confidence in God, your season has arrived.

REFLECTION:

June 19

"Is there no balm in Gilead, Is there no physician there? Why then has not the health of the daughter of my people been restored?" (Jeremiah 8:22 New American Standard).

I don't know how you view this question, but many people see it as sort of a rhetorical question. The people of God should always have the benefit of the ultimate Physician. The problem then was the same as the problem now: SIN! God wants to tremendously bless all of His people. In the days of Jeremiah, God sent him to express His anguish over their choices. Why would anyone with God on their side want someone else in their corner? The Bible is really a collection of writings about God's desire to have a relationship with mankind. We try to make it much more complicated than that, but the common thread is God's appeal to be accepted and appreciated. Even today God provides for us, rebukes the enemy for us, opens doors for us, invents positions for us, and keeps us sane. Yet, when the slightest thing goes awry, we tend to come apart and act like God just owes us His goodness. The balm in Gilead will heal with greater than prescription strength once we obey the voice of God.

REFLECTION:

June 20

"Joanna, the wife of Chuza, Herod's business manager; Susanna; and many others who were contributing from their own resources to support Jesus and his disciples" (Luke 8:3 New Living Translation).

I can't speak for you, but I find this a very fascinating verse that I have overlooked and have never heard anyone make mention of it. Wasn't Herod one of the Lord's biggest adversaries? I believe the Scripture mentions things and details deliberately. The message of Jesus apparently penetrated the lives of His biggest opponents. Does that happen when we share the gospel? I get the impression that we share Christ in a way that tries to make people appreciate us instead of challenging them to love Him.

Another thing that stands out is how this verse mentions women personally supporting Him. As much as I hate to admit it, our sisters show a profound appreciation for the gospel ministry and demonstrate it in meaningful and lasting ways. Anyone whose life has been forever changed by the gospel shouldn't mind ministering to Him from their own resources. We aren't doing God a favor when we give. We aren't doing the preacher a favor when we give either. Most of us waste more than we invest. Is there any greater investment than the transformation of lives?

REFLECTION:

June 21

"And as they went to tell his disciples, behold, Jesus met them, saying, all hail. And they came and held him by the feet and worshipped him" (Matthew 28:9 King James Version).

The tomb was empty! The problem is that countless hearts and lives were likewise empty. Even though Jesus did all He could to prepare His devotees for His death, it was still difficult to comprehend how someone with that much power, that much influence, and that close to God could leave without immediately setting up His kingdom. The people of God were starving for deliverance. Even in the life of Jesus, the powers persecuted the Jews. Just when they thought relief had finally come, He died at the very hands of those they expected Him to overcome.

In the verse above, Jesus met those who visited the empty tomb while they were going to give His other disciples word that his body was gone. "All hail" was a declaration of supreme authority. It was the comfort they needed to endure whatever His plan called for. His emergence after death told them that everything they experienced was God's plan for ultimate and permanent deliverance. They didn't realize it, but death was a bigger adversary than Rome. If Jesus had not appeared victorious, they wouldn't have had the courage to live and die for Him. Worship the Lord. All power in heaven and earth is His!

REFLECTION:

June 22

"This report concerning Him went out all over Judea and in all the surrounding district" (Luke 7:17 New American Standard).

Sometimes you read a verse and wonder, *What in the world is this verse talking about?* Although these devotions are based on one verse, the ideas are based on the entire story told in multiple verses. Jesus raised the only son of a widow from the dead. So, she had already lost her husband. Then, she lost her son. It appeared as though the entire village supported her. Don't allow yourself to doubt if God cares what you're going through. True: it isn't always God's response to act in this manner. I believe the point of this and other Bible accounts is to demonstrate the compassion of God.

Our gratitude should be that God decides to act at all. Now the report concerning Jesus was that He was a great prophet and that God had visited His people. Somewhere as the centuries passed, God's people began to live as though we can obligate God to do as we demand. God is sovereign, and He knows what to do, when to do it, and why He is doing it! Are you grateful for a visitation even when it isn't your situation that gets addressed? When we learn to walk others through their valleys, we will be better equipped to appreciate every move of God.

REFLECTION:

June 23

"THERE IS NO FEAR OF GOD BEFORE THEIR EYES" (Romans 3:18 New American Standard).

This is one of those verses that this version put in all caps in order to add emphasis. Some people commit a grievous error by treating the grace of God as a license to live in unrighteousness. Anyone who doesn't feel any remorse when the Spirit is compelling them to walk with God doesn't have a genuine relationship with Him. If there is no fear of God that prevents you from certain behavior, you really have to examine yourself. The fear of God is not a restrictive terror that forces you to do acceptable things. The fear of the Lord is that which guides you safely through all of the issues of life.

Whether we are talking about individuals or entire nations, all of us will answer to God. All of us have an opportunity to consider before we act. When you consider, you are attempting to look into the future beyond your decision. In other words, you have to ask yourself, *Are the consequences of this decision something I can handle for the rest of my life?* Sometimes a decision carries lifetime implications that change you forever. Make your decisions with the fear of the Lord in front of you, rather than endless regret behind you.

REFLECTION:

June 24

"Wherefore thou art no more a servant, but a son; and if a son, then an heir of God through Christ" (Galatians 4:7 King James Version).

Often times you will hear people refer to themselves as servants of the Lord. I believe this is commendable, and when authentic, it is a sign of humility. Servants remind themselves that the Master's goodness is an undeserved blessing. I don't have anything contrary to say to anyone that calls themselves a servant of the Lord. I only want to ask that you keep that humble attitude when you realize that you are better than a servant of the Lord. You are a SON of God. The daughters of God are also included in the term sons of God. You will rarely hear of a servant that is regarded as an heir.

Servants were honored whenever the master decided to bestow honor. But all of the honor bestowed didn't give you access to the estate. God has given His children equal access to His unlimited resources. Another blessing is that He doesn't require you to die before you start to enjoy His benefits. You don't become a greater child when you die. John told us that we are sons of God right now! If we could adequately comprehend what it means to be God's beneficiary, we wouldn't stress out nearly as often.

REFLECTION:

June 25

"This command I entrust to you, Timothy, my son, in accordance the prophecies previously made concerning you, that by them you fight the good fight" (I Timothy 1:18 NKJV).

I don't know about you, but if I were Timothy, I would probably feel quite humbled by the charges Paul gave. I would also feel a great sense of spiritual pressure to carry on the next generation of his ministry. The scriptures don't really tell us how things turned out for Timothy. One of the interesting contrasts between the Old and New Testaments is that we don't really hear much about New Testament failures. The New Testament gives us major instructions for spiritual living, both as individuals and as collective congregations. This particular charge involved keeping the faith with a pure conscience.

If Timothy followed the encouraging instructions of Paul, I'm sure he had a successful ministry. It is a great challenge to discipline yourself in such a way that your conscience is clear. Success in God's eyes has little to do with your public performance. God wants to be pleased when the doors are closed and when the audience is only Him.

REFLECTION:

_____

_____

_____

_____

_____

_____

_____

_____

_____

_____

_____

June 26

"Then I will purify the lips of the peoples, that all of them may call on the name of the Lord and serve him shoulder to shoulder" (Zephaniah 3:9 New International Version).

After the purging of the rebellious, God gets involved in the uniting of those serving Him. It's impossible to have complete unity when the God-haters are still around. The purifying of the lips speaks of everyone saying the same thing. The people of God should all be saying the SAME thing! Serving God shoulder to shoulder gives a military context of a formation. When we stand side by side, nothing can come between us. There is no separation or gaps for the enemy to sneak through. The ones standing together should be about the same height to eliminate a picture of weakness. The shorter, younger, and weaker ones should be standing behind the protective wall of front-line servants. When God takes up your cause, feel sorry for anyone standing in His way!

REFLECTION:

June 27

"But even if we or an angel from heaven should preach to you a gospel contrary to the one we preached to you, let him be accursed" (Galatians 1:8 English Standard Version).

This is one of those statements that proves Paul wasn't just trying to advance his own personal agenda. If someone is willing to disqualify themselves, they aren't carrying their own message. The gospel is just that precious. There is only one truth. The truth doesn't change according to our desire to believe something. Even if you hear an angel that wants to update or amend the message that came from the mouth of Jesus, don't believe it.

You would be surprised to learn just how much the original message has already been amended by scoffers. The gospel is both simple and yet profound. Christ died for our sins. He was buried. He was raised on the third day, and He was observed and proven to be alive! If anyone has anything else to say that would refute or diminish that message, Paul says they should be literally cut off from the presence of the Lord at His return. God has only one plan for all mankind. He doesn't need any of us trying to improve it. It worked from the beginning, and it still works today.

REFLECTION:

June 28

"Fight the good fight of the faith. Take hold of the eternal life to which you were called and about which you made the good confession in the presence of many witnesses" (I Timothy 6:12 English Standard Version).

Even if your personality is non-confrontational, your faith ought to be very confrontational. I'm tired of God's people watering down their beliefs just to be liked and accepted by those who care nothing about our God. Most of us care more about what celebrities think than what God thinks. There is a fine line between being all things to all people and doing anything for the respect of all people. If your message becomes dim to the person that needs the light, you have compromised your position.

Timothy was commended for a good profession despite being criticized for his timid personality. God will stand up in you if you agree to stand up for Him. The good fight is indicative of the burden God places upon His servants. Once He calls you, the fight ensues. You don't have to do anything to instigate the fight. The fact that God loves you is enough to make you hated in the world and in the demonic realm. Since God requires us to fight, He must be expecting conflict. If God is expecting conflict, why don't we? Your faith fights for God, and God fights for you.

REFLECTION:

June 29

"We must work the works of him who sent me while it is day; night is coming when no one can work" (John 9:4 English Standard Version).

Some versions say, "I must work...," while this version says: "we must work." It is a small difference, but I think it is a difference worth pointing out. The ministry of Jesus was always inclusive. He didn't start doing ministry until He had selected those who would carry on the ministry after Him. He came to seek and to save those who were lost. He came to die for the sin of the entire world of all time. Jesus understood that He only had a limited window of opportunity to complete the task assigned by God.

We all have a "daytime" chance to serve God for the benefit of the kingdom. The two-fold mission each of us has is to fulfill the mandate placed on us by God and to pour ourselves in a significant fashion into at least one other person. When Jesus talks about night, He is referring to a time when it will be too late to finish your course. Now it is imperative that we do the works of Him that sent Jesus. Jesus said "we" because God gave Him a task that was beyond accomplishment all alone. God has also given YOU something that you can't do all alone.

REFLECTION:

June 30

"Then I thought in my heart, 'The fate of the fool will overtake me also. What then do I gain by being wise?' I said in my heart, 'This too is meaningless'" (Ecclesiastes 2:15 New International Version).

Praying in the Spirit and being alert demands that you have the discernment to sense the will of God and prioritize it. We must be diligent to pray for ALL the saints, not just the ones in your church, your sister churches, and your denomination. Jesus assumes we will give, we will fast, and we will pray. If God can't count on us for things He assumes we will do, how can we "expect" Him to take action in our circumstances?

REFLECTION:

JULY

July 1

"But though we had already suffered and been shamefully treated at Philippi, as you know, we had boldness in our God to declare to you the gospel of God in the midst of much conflict" (I Thessalonians 2:2 English Standard Version).

When people see how much you're willing to suffer for your cause, they are usually much more willing to at least listen. Unfortunately, suffering is a reality in this life. Many of us suffer as quiet Christians while Paul suffered because of his call. Sometimes we think boldness means that we will declare the gospel in a dark environment. Paul's kind of boldness is characterized by continuing to declare after you have already endured persecution. A hostile environment doesn't mean you will be persecuted. These believers knew firsthand that Paul was slandered, beaten, deserted, and exposed.

When Paul had an opportunity the preach the gospel, he considered it an honor to suffer for Christ. Most of us won't even suffer with Him, let alone suffer for Him. Paul had the resolve to go through conflict for any person in need of salvation. Do you think you could plan your next preaching engagement after being hospitalized for the beating you took the last time you preached?

REFLECTION:

_____

_____

_____

_____

_____

_____

_____

_____

_____

July 2

"This includes you who were once far away from God. You were his enemies, separated from him by your evil thought and actions" (Colossians 1:21 New Living Translation).

Paul doesn't have a problem putting all of us in the same boat. Many people try to justify themselves before God because they manage to do good and humane works. But notice how Paul first mentioned thoughts. I don't care how holy you claim to be; your thoughts are regularly contrary to the holy nature of God. It is good to prevent less than wholesome things from proceeding out of your mouth, but you wouldn't have to prevent them if they weren't first in your mind. It would startle us to truly know just how far away from God we were. The real point of this verse is how we were included in those who were enemies of God.

You wouldn't be very popular these days if you told people they were God's enemies. We must be bold enough to present the real truth of the gospel. What good would it do to make people feel good about themselves, only to die without Christ? The goal is to get the truth to them without being aloof or deceptive. How often do we wonder where our acquaintances will spend eternity? Thank God Paul said we "were" in a bad state. Now in Christ we have the security of everlasting safety.

REFLECTION:

July 3

"For He established a testimony in Jacob and appointed a law in Israel, which He commanded our fathers that they should teach them to their children" (Psalms 78:5 New American Standard).

This psalm was written to magnify the importance of the commandments of God. The thoughts and wishes of God should be important to everyone. To the people of God, the thoughts and wishes of God are like breath. Stop right now and try to imagine your life without the word of God. You can't even comprehend that, can you? When God speaks, things are established. When God speaks, law has just been born.

Many of us try to leave a financial legacy for our children and grandchildren. We also try to at least finance their education. Here is an education that doesn't cost a dime! I'm certainly not suggesting that we neglect a financial legacy or the importance of higher learning. However, why don't we give more regard to godly legacies? Teaching our children about God will help them go through life armed with wisdom and understanding. If properly prepared, you can handle any situation life throws at you. Without proper preparation, all the money and all the education in the world won't guarantee success.

REFLECTION:

July 4

"For where a will is involved, the death of the one who made it must be established" (Hebrews 9:16 English Standard Version).

The will of God has always required blood in order to be in force. Even in the Old Testament, the blood of Christ was the only satisfying component God would accept. So, the obvious question is, "How were any of the Old Testament sacrifices accepted when Christ didn't come until the New Testament?" The answer is not so obvious unless you understand spiritual principles. God accepted the blood sacrifices before Christ because He accepted them on the future merit of Jesus' blood. Now here is where it gets a bit technical but spiritual. The Bible clearly teaches that Christ was slain before the world began. In other words, He died for the world and the inhabitants of the world before God even made the world! Because of that, the blood sacrifices in the Old Testament were actually after the death of Christ, but before His human sacrifice in time. God is eternal and exists outside of time. Because He is God, He can step into time whenever He pleases. The death of Christ is a proven fact: the proof is our Salvation and the seal and work of the Holy Spirit.

REFLECTION:

July 5

"And now in these final days, he has spoken to us through his Son. God promised everything to the Son as an inheritance, and through the Son he created the universe" (Hebrews 1:2 New Living Translation).

If God has anything to say at all, He says it through Jesus. He is the satisfaction of the Law and the fulfillment of the prophets. Everything has its origins in Him, and everything comes to completion in Him. Everything alive needs Him to exist, and every universal system of organization consists in Him. Jesus is the Word of God. That might not be news to many of you, but it should be a reminder to us that we can't neglect His word and expect to be successful in anything. Although we should memorize the word, we can't rely on the memorized word to carry us through our days.

You need a healthy dose of scripture on a daily basis the same way you need food and water on a daily basis. Many of us have loved ones that we speak to very often, if not every day. Do we consider God our loved One that we need to speak to regularly? Maybe we struggle with this because we forget that God is a PERSON. He has feelings, joys, sorrows, plans for us, hopes for us, and desires for us. He forfeited everything to give us everything. Why benefit from His strength and disregard Him?

REFLECTION:

July 6

"But it is not as though the word of God has failed. For not all who are descended from Israel belong to Israel" (Romans 9:6 English Standard Version).

Paul does a masterful job at explaining the depth of God's promises. The promises God gave Israel extended to the spiritual seed of Abraham through Isaac. In other words, there are descendants of Abraham, Isaac, and Jacob (Israel) that won't qualify for the promises to be fulfilled in them. I can see that some of you are still a bit confused about this scenario.

Many descendants of the patriarchs perished in the wilderness because of unbelief. These were literal children of Israel. The promises of God to deliver Israel pertained to those who believed God the same way Abraham believed God. Every one that made it through the test of the wilderness was delivered because they believed God through faith. The word God gave Abraham never failed. The word God gives us never fails either. If you see a promise in the word of God that didn't come to pass in your life, it means that promise wasn't made to you! We have to know when God is talking to us or when God is talking for us. If there is a disconnect, the problem is with us, not with God.

REFLECTION:

July 7

"And after you have suffered a little while, the God of all grace, who has called you to his eternal glory in Christ, will himself restore, confirm, strengthen, and establish you" (I Peter 5:10 English Standard Version).

Peter is a seasoned veteran at this point in his life and walk. He certainly pulled from every remembrance of Jesus' teachings when he wrote this letter. You can hear Peter s gratitude for being accepted by the God of all grace. Peter's words outline the process for the household of faith. Suffering always accompanies an honest walk with God. If you haven't suffered yet, expect it. God never leaves you without a context for your suffering. I didn't say He would give you an explanation, I said He will give you a context. He uses it to perFECT you. You're not perfect, but you're being perFECTED! Once you can be trusted, He then establishes you. If He didn't do it in this manner, you might start an ego trip when He establishes you. Giving you strength is the next step in the process because people will start to respond with envy. Finally, He settles you so that no one will be able to uproot what He has invested in you. No matter where you are in this process right now, trust the God of all grace. His plan is proceeding according to plan. Once you cross the finish line in THIS race, you will be a completed vessel.

REFLECTION:

July 8

"Dear brothers and sisters, if another believer is overcome by some sin, you who are godly should gently and humbly help that person back onto the right path. And be careful not to fall into the same temptation yourself" (Galatians 6:1 New Living Translation).

I like this translation because it doesn't assume everyone spiritual is godly. Other translations say that a spiritual person should restore, but many readers don't look up the meaning of spiritual. Just because you go to church regularly, and you mean no harm, it doesn't qualify you for the ministry of restoration. I have also observed that most people in the restoration ministry act alone. I think it is tragic to engage in any level of spiritual warfare alone.

When you witness to unbelievers, you shouldn't be alone. When you minister to believers, you shouldn't be alone either. It will probably take a consistent and prayerful approach, but God helps you avoid the temptation when you have a prayer partner. You need a strategy because most of us tend to justify our behavior and minimize weaknesses. Most of the time the person will talk about their strong points and treat the weakness as no big deal. The intensity of the intervention will depend on how the person feels about what's going on and how much they care about who's affected.

REFLECTION:

July 9

"Then he answered and said to me, 'This is the word of the Lord to Zerubbabel saying, Not by might nor by power, but by my Spirit,' says the Lord of hosts'" (Zechariah 4:6 New American Standard).

This word from the Lord came as the result of a vision. Many people pride themselves on their connections to people of influence. God makes it clear that you need the leading of His Spirit to do exploits on earth. Political clout is good, but God doesn't need it. Religious affiliations are good, but God doesn't need them. Any combination of earthly might and power doesn't impress God in the least. He needs FAITH to do mighty works. No matter what the question is; the answer is found in the Spirit of the Lord of hosts. He is Almighty and All-powerful!

REFLECTION:

July 10

"For if we sin willfully after that we have received the knowledge of the truth, there remaineth no more sacrifice for sins" (Hebrews 10:26 King James Version).

The child of God should have undergone a transformation. For us to continue in a LIFESTYLE of decadence after receiving the good news of the gospel says we have really remained the same. This isn't about your profession but your possession. If we say, "Not my will, but thy will be done," how can we find ourselves constantly entangled in our own will? Jesus is the only acceptable sacrifice. So, if He isn't enough for us to lay down our own plans, there isn't ANY other plan! Therefore, no other sacrifice is possible. We will always have some actions that are questionable, but no Christian should be living a questionable lifestyle. If anyone is in Christ, you are a NEW creation.

REFLECTION:

July 11

"For we are not, as so many, peddling the word of God; but as of sincerity, but as from God, we speak in the sight of God in Christ" (II Corinthians 2:17 New King James Version).

Just imagine what must be happening in our day if Paul felt the word of God was peddled in his day. We have reality shows, lifestyles that boast power with no demonstration, and an environment where the lost and saved look identical. I seriously think people forget that God will hold us accountable for what we compel people to believe. How can anyone say they love God while manipulating His people with His word?

Paul often showed the difference between the authentic and the imposter. The real difference is that God will always support His word. From the Old Testament to the New Testament, God looked after His word to perform it. The word of God will ALWAYS accomplish the purposes of God. The church and the world would be in much better shape if we all spoke as though God was recording every word. I believe that is how Paul was able to exercise such self-control because he recognized that everything he did was in God's sight. To do all things as unto the Lord will give us the mental edge we need to resist the urge to take advantage of anyone. God is their advocate, so handle them with care.

REFLECTION:

July 12

"Through faith also Sara herself received strength to conceive seed and was delivered of a child when she was past age, because she judged him faithful who had promised" (Hebrews 11:11 King James Version).

Sometimes the word of God speaks of things happening "through" faith, and sometimes "by" faith. Maybe I'm splitting hairs, but I believe "through" faith gives a different kind of glory to Jesus because the life we live is through His faith. Paul knew that he couldn't live without God living through him. Imagine what you can do if you really grasp that Jesus wants to operate His faith through you.

Sara was able to have the faith-child that she actually laughed about at one time. Even when we deny God, He can't deny Himself because He is faithful. We have to understand that God can do ANYTHING He wants to do. God can use ANYONE He wants to use. He can bring His will to pass ANYWHERE He chooses.

What does God want to bring into this world through you? Everyone else may think your time is past, but times and seasons belong to God and God alone. Lock into the promise of God and watch Him defy logic, silence the doubters, and absolutely blow your mind.

REFLECTION:

July 13

"For Christ himself has brought peace to us. He united Jews and Gentiles into one people when, in his own body on the cross, he broke down the wall of hostility that separated us" (Ephesians 2:14 New Living Translation).

There are many other benefits from the death of Christ that people don't really talk about. God's intent in the earth has always been oneness. Walls and various tools of division have been the tactics of Satan ever since the Garden of Eden. Christ paid the ultimate price for every kind of sin. Throughout human history, many have been deceived by thinking God made people either inferior or superior to other people. Christ not only taught peace and preached peace, He modeled peace.

How bad do you want walls to come down in your environment? Ancient cities were built with the idea of separation. A city that had high and wide walls was considered impenetrable. However, if we could get along as individuals, there would be no need to hide behind these false security measures. Hostility has been dealt with completely and effectively. All we have to do is let the Holy Spirit reshape our thinking. Christ believed everyone was valuable.

REFLECTION:

July 14

"He answered and said, Lo, I see four men loose, walking in the midst of the fire, and they have no hurt; and the form of the fourth is like the Son of God" (Daniel 3:25 King James Version).

In the Bible, fire is a picture of judgment. In this case, the integrity of the Hebrew boys made God "escort" them through the hottest time in their lives. We are told not to fear them that can only destroy the body but fear Him that can destroy both body and soul in hell's fire. Man's fire is like a walk in the park to God. In reality, He uses this as an opportunity to get a pagan king's attention. When your ways please God, He will make even your enemies be at peace with you. When your trials are seven times hotter than ever, He will be there to free you. When the world looks at you, you too can "HAVE NO HURT!"

REFLECTION:

July 15

"Therefore, do not be ashamed of the testimony of our Lord or of me His prisoner, but join with me in suffering for the gospel according to the power of God" (II Timothy 1:8 New American Standard).

When we are ashamed to speak up for the Lord, it is a direct result of fear. Remember the last verse told us that God hasn't given us the spirit of fear. How does fear manifest itself in keeping us from speaking up? We fear that we won't fit in with a crowd. We fear that a person will ridicule us and consider us a religious fanatic or a Jesus freak. We fear that we can't respond if a person raises a good question. We fear that a rough-looking person won't desire to hear our testimony. We fear that something a person knows about us will make us a hypocrite. Do any of these sound familiar? The power of God is absent in a of those responses and then some. Paul tells Timothy to join him in suffering for the gospel. How often does the average Christian mention Christ outside of a church gathering or setting? Trust me: I'm also telling on myself. Being a pastor helps me talk about it because it's my life. The challenge is not to be ashamed because we don't want Him to be ashamed of us.

REFLECTION:

July 16

"For by him all things were created, in heaven and on earth, visible and invisible, whether thrones or dominions or rulers or authorities—all things were created through him and for him" (Colossians 1:16 English Standard Version).

Let me remind all of us of one very important point: GOD is in charge of everything! So many times, we get concerned about the power of government, the reputation of institutions, and the terror of tyrants. However, God still has His hand over all of them. Your life was given to you in the hope that you would give it back to God. Before you get alarmed about that, God works in your favor when He can be glorified from your life. Even invisible things were designed to honor God.

Problems come in when we decide to chart our own course and become the masters of our own destiny. You can't be the master of anything that isn't under your control. Everything we do is by permission. God called a man foolish because he presumed he would be able to build bigger barns to house his blessings. He was foolish because he wasn't aware that he wouldn't live through the night. We will all finish life one day, but at least we will be eternally grateful for having lived in light of God's pleasure. Even those who rebel against God were originally created to glorify God. Unfortunately, many have decided to ignore their original purpose.

REFLECTION:

July 17

"And they sang a new song: You are worthy to take the scroll and to open its seals, because you were slain, and with your blood you purchased men for God from every tribe and language and people and nation" (Revelation 5:9 New International Version).

The blood of Christ is international, even universal. His sacrifice has exalted Him to a unique position, giving Him unprecedented authority. When God is pleased, He looks to show His satisfaction in the most beneficial and lasting way. The purchase price for humanity was infinite because we were sold in sin. The greatest "addiction" in the flesh is its obsession and compulsion to dishonor God. By giving His life, Christ DESTROYED the grip of sin on mankind. With Him, you have a choice. God gives His power to anyone who prays for it. God is not willing that any person perish. There will be people forgiven from all over the world. Ask and receive. Seek and find. Knock and have the door opened to you. Someone owns you. Why not let it be God?

REFLECTION:

July 18

"Now if Christ is preached that He has been raised from the dead, how do some among you say that there is no resurrection of the dead?" (I Corinthians 15:12 King James Version).

The word we preach and the word we believe has been confirmed by countless witnesses. If it could be proved that anything Christ claimed was false, wouldn't the devil have found a way to exploit it? Even if you don't believe in the devil, the plan would be to discredit Christ. Countless millions of followers have based their faith on the truth of the resurrection. Generations have preached the truth in the empty tomb of Jesus. Why would anyone try to say that Jesus didn't rise from the dead? The only apparent reason is to try and draw away followers for themselves.

God knows how to confirm His word. No power will be able to prove anything wrong in scripture. Many have attempted to use "logic" to make us wonder whether the Bible is true. Logically speaking, a whale wouldn't swallow a person and that same person live to testify. Logically speaking, the sun wouldn't stand still in order to assist a man in battle. Logically speaking, someone would never rise from the dead and ascend to heaven. Good thing God isn't confined by human logic.

REFLECTION:

July 19

"Consequently, you are no longer foreigners and strangers, but fellow citizens with God's people and also members of his household" (Ephesians 2:19 New International Version).

The work of Christ on the cross gave us access to God. That is what this verse means by "consequently." There are many things afforded us by the sacrificial, atoning, and vicarous death of Christ. As Gentiles, we were initially excluded from the benefits of favor with God. But now the veil has been torn, the wall of partition has been demolished, and we have the same privileges as God's original chosen people. When you think about it, Jesus made it clear that His followers didn't choose Him; He chose them. God wants everyone, but not everyone will respond to His invitation. Only God can make a relative out of a foreigner. Only God can transform tares into wheat. Only God can make a citizen of someone who was formerly an enemy. I know we don't like to admit that we were literal enemies of God, but that's what God says we were. We have been invited to the table to dine with God, fellowship with God, rule with God, and ultimately reign with God. Not bad for someone who was once His enemy.

REFLECTION:

July 20

"Fear the LORD, you his saints, for those who fear him lack nothing" (Psalms 34:9 New International Version).

The word "fear" in this verse means to stand in awe, to cause astonishment, and to inspire reverence and godly fear or respect. Who would be better qualified to fear the Lord than the saints? We have an established relationship with Him, so we should be a shining testimony of the benefits in fearing the Lord. If you fear the Lord, you will obey Him. If you fear the Lord, you will honor Him. If you fear the Lord, you will be careful to represent Him properly. People will never see God, but what they see in you should tell them a lot about Him. The last part of this verse promises that He will take care of those who fear Him.

Paul followed up in the New Testament by telling us that God will supply every need according to His riches in glory. When your confidence is in God, you can sleep at night. Actually, you can sleep pretty good in the daytime, too. David experienced enough to know the goodness of God in spite of the wickedness of the flesh. Although we aren't always model children, He is always the ideal Father.

REFLECTION:

July 21

"Therefore, whoever resists the authorities resists what God has appointed, and those who resist will incur judgment" (Romans 13:2 English Standard Version).

Yes, we live in a free country where government officials are said to be public servants. Many of us believe we decide who does what and for how long. God says He sets up some and sets down others. Look at it like this; churches believe they vote in leaders. Actually, God does the calling, the assigning, and the ordaining. Then, He allows us to pretend we had the power.

Throughout the entire Old Testament, God would raise up leaders to be a tool of blessing or a tool of chastisement. I happen to believe the entire world functions according to the rapport God's people have with Him. And if you look at the message of Christ to the churches in Revelation, He always talked about their condition first before talking about what the enemies of the gospel were up to. It really doesn't matter what unbelievers are doing. When the Son of man comes, will He find faith on the earth? When we resist delegated authority, we resist the One that delegated the authority, too. No one has ever gotten away with snubbing God.

REFLECTION:

July 22

"When neither sun nor stars appeared for many days, and no small tempest lay on us, all hope of our lives being saved was at last abandoned" (Acts 27:20 English Standard Version).

This is a small part of the account of Paul's voyage to Italy. I can't speak for you, but I sometimes wonder how long God will see fit to use me. This was a serious and dangerous storm that had everyone on board fearing for their lives. Even children of God don't always know what God intends to do. A personal storm that hides the "light" of His presence for an extended period can be very frightening. Besides that, the tempest beat on them in the midst of their darkness.

It seems as though you're all alone when the storm is raging. I believe God wants us to depend completely on Him at critical times. Did you realize that God still directs you even when you lose all hope? There will be numerous times in your walk when you will wish you could tell God how to deliver you. God reserves the right to use your storms any way He pleases, for as long as He pleases, to teach you something that He can't show you any other way. Difficulty gets our attention in unique ways. God saved everyone on board the ship but not the ship. Storms train your attitude for the next assignment.

REFLECTION:

July 23

"They said to you, 'In the last times there will be scoffers who will follow their own ungodly desires'" (Jude 18 New International Version).

The apostles of Jesus warned the followers of God about conditions in the last days. This proves the disciples finally got the message Jesus continually tried to give them. One of the ministries of the Holy Spirit is to remind us of what Jesus said. Therefore, the apostles were the first to benefit when the day of Pentecost came, ushering in the age of the Holy Spirit. The Spirit of God does the same thing for us. We need to be reminded what the bible says as we engage in spiritual warfare.

Scoffers feel as though they need to attack the message of Christ so they can promote their own agenda. Why can't they just go ahead and follow their own ungodly desires? It appears some groups want to force God into defending Himself. When the sky doesn't fall on them for their arrogance, they assume to dismiss the bible as untrue. God doesn't need to justify His existence under their terms. He doesn't need to justify His existence at all. The only thing these scoffers accomplish is building up a huge pile of wrath to be reckoned with on judgement day.

REFLECTION:

July 24

"David also said, 'As the LORD lives, surely the LORD will strike him, or his day will come that he dies, or he will go down into battle and perish'" (I Samuel 26:10 New American Standard).

David had the perfect opportunity to take Saul's life. Abishai pleaded with David for the chance to execute Saul, yet David decided to keep running from him. It even looked as though God made it right for David to make his move and terminate his biggest enemy. After all, God had chosen David to replace Saul, and David didn't do anything worthy of Saul's hatred. Do you think you could continue to run from an enemy that seeks your life, and leave it up to God to deal with him?

David is demonstrating tremendous faith, and he is trusting God to exact vengeance. David was not known for being a prophet, yet he showed unusual insight into the plan of God. Many of us can discern the good coming our way because of God's promises. Yet, the biggest struggle is waiting until the time has come for His promises to manifest. David ran for many years before God established him. I also believe David knew it would be difficult to be king of Judah and Israel had he murdered the people's choice.

REFLECTION:

July 25

"They will act religious, but they will reject the power that could make them godly. Stay away from people like that" (II Timothy 3:5 New Living Translation).

How many people do you know that fits this description? Would anyone else reading this put your name on their list? I certainly hope not! Paul was very clear in some of his other letters that true followers of Christ walk with a demonstration of Holy Ghost power. Anyone can shout, cry, dance, and fall out. The thing that matters most is how much of your will does God possess? You can be a child of God and not give Him access to your stubborn will. Every child of God is not godly. Just like every child of yours doesn't always act like you. In some cases, that might not be such a bad thing. I'm just kidding; don't be so sensitive. What a tragedy to reject the power of God in your life that only has the motive of making you godly.

People can see through a religious veneer the same way they can see through a glass. If you went to see a doctor that was constantly talking about successful treatments for patients, but you never saw any evidence of their success, how much confidence would you have to lay on their table? Stop bragging about the power of God and silently demonstrate it.

REFLECTION:

July 26

"For we are the circumcision, who worship by the Spirit of God and glory in Christ Jesus and put no confidence in the flesh." (Philippians 3:3 English Standard Version).

This is one example of the Spirit of God being mentioned along with worship. Jesus told the woman at the well that God is seeking worshipers. He is seeking those who will worship Him in Spirit and in truth. Since the Bible included the Spirit of God in the worship of God, we should look a bit deeper for further clarification. The Spirit of God is the One that informs us of all things concerning God. The Spirit of God interprets our prayers according to the will of God. We wouldn't have a relationship with God apart from the Spirit of God. We wouldn't be placed into the body of Christ apart from the Spirit of God. He reveals the mind of God to us. Once we are allowed to "comprehend" God by His Spirit, we can intelligently submit, sacrifice, and serve.

When we walk with God according to what God reveals to us about Him, we are allowed to enter a worship experience. There is no formula for worship. It is extremely difficult to define it. When God overwhelms you by His presence and His pleasure, nothing else matters. If anything has clouded His importance, keep pressing in.

REFLECTION:

July 27

"And he began to teach them that the Son of Man must suffer many things and be rejected by the elders and chief priests and scribes, and be killed, and after three days rise again" (Mark 8:31 New King James Version).

Jesus always knew when to introduce a new thought to His disciples. Whenever Jesus discusses something, revelation is the result. The disciples tended to move out thinking they really knew their Savior. We too presume to think we have arrived in a certain area, only to find out we have to go back to Him for deeper instructions. Teaching will always be necessary to take the next step in your walk with God. Teaching is also done in doses. We have to learn the fellowship of His suffering. We can never truly comprehend it, but we must attempt to investigate it.

The greatest "religious" figure of all time was preparing to be rejected by the leaders of those He came to save. Not only would He be rejected, but it would also be determined that He isn't even fit to live after all He had done. But hold on, the story isn't over because He would rise from the dead three days later. This had to be taught because logic could never see it as the will of God. The only thing worth living for is to KNOW HIM! As we grow in knowledge, we understand grace more, too.

REFLECTION:

July 28

"These people honor me with their lips, but their hearts are far from me" (Matthew 15:8 New International Version).

Jesus had this response observing how these religious people approached the Law. You can't have a quality relationship with anyone if you are only committed with your words and dedicated in the face of public scrutiny. Jesus compared what their lips proclaimed to the content of their hearts. I believe He is still doing that today. We all know what to say. It is no big deal to say what people want to hear. The beauty of a relationship is when you are committed to doing what pleases the other party.

People seem more interested in having a relationship with religion than with a person. They didn't even understand the Spirit behind the Law. I also find it quite interesting that no one really uses this verse to accuse Jesus of claiming equality with God. For Jesus to say that people are drawing near to "Me" with their heart is a clear indication that He is accepting honor and homage that would ordinarily be reserved for God. The real tragedy is that their behavior is only superficial. God deserves much more than just a surface and perfunctory allegiance.

REFLECTION:

July 29

"Not everyone who says to me, 'Lord, Lord,' will enter the kingdom of heaven, but the one whc does the will of my Father who is in heaven" (Matthew 7:21 English Standa-d Version).

As you can see, there's more to establishing a kingdom than saying the right words. Jesus lived a sacrificial life in order to show us what kingdom citizens look like, sound like, and behave like. You may be sitting next to church members, but there s no guarantee you're sitting next to God's children. This portion of Matthew was dedicated to teaching the disciples how to live. Jesus talked about the straight gate, false prophets, the kind of fruit a tree produces, and many other foundational elements. Actually, most of the text is red in chapters 5-7 of Matthew. If there's one thing that upsets God's stomach, it's hypocrisy. If you really want to glorify God, you will DO something.

Let me ask you a question that requires thought, "Can you really glorify God with words alone?" Doing the will of the Father implies action. There would be no point in teaching if there was no expectation of change. The kingdom of heaven will be inhabited by changed individuals that sacrifice their own will for God's will.

REFLECTION:

July 30

"These things I have spoken to you, that my joy may be in you, and that your joy may be full" (John 15:11 English Standard Version).

You can't possibly hope to be anything like Jesus unless you allow His words to permeate your being. He says what He says so that we can learn to do what's necessary for a fulfilling life according to His standards. Can you remember how you felt when the joy of the Lord was evident in you? There's a sense of invincibility that keeps you moving forward, not a sense of arrogance but a true sense of confidence. His joy in you keeps you hopeful. The fullness of joy keeps you useful.

God can't work through you without first working in you. If you are filled with joy, there's no room for anything else. You can have joy even in dire straits. You can have joy when happiness has escaped you. You can have joy when you see it as a gift of grace. When we get accustomed to things going well, we can take God for granted. We aren't entitled to anything. Yet, He has chosen to give us everything. Joy comes at the remembrance of His goodness.

REFLECTION:

July 31

"Beloved, if our heart does not condemn us, we have confidence before God" (1 John 3:21 English Standard Version).

Examining the heart can be a very tricky ordeal. Since God is the only One that can accurately assess the condition of the heart, we must rely on what He reveals about it. Another verse tells us if the heart condemns us, God is greater and knows everything. God will communicate to you through your spirit. Your spirit will convict your heart according to the desires of the Holy Spirit. I don't want to get complicated, so just know that God has a way of letting you know when He is pleased and when He is not. The confidence we have in God has nothing to do with good works. The confidence we have towards God is a result of a good relationship and good fellowship. The confidence we have leads us to pray, letting our requests be made known to Him. He hears us and grants the requests because we keep His commandments and do things that please Him. God wants us to remain close to Him. We remain close to Him by resisting the pull of the flesh. God always wants to answer our prayers. Let Him examine your heart so He can tell you how to proceed in dealing with Him, with life, and with everyone else.

REFLECTION:

AUGUST

August 1

"All they knew was that people were saying, 'The one who used to persecute us is now preaching the very faith he tried to destroy'" (Galatians 1:23 New Living Translation).

In this portion of Galatians, Paul is confirming his apostleship. When the Lord called him, he didn't get any confirmation from anyone. He didn't even confer with the other apostles. He only spent time with Peter after some years went by. That in itself is fairly interesting, especially in light of the fact that there was quite a meeting when Judas needed to be replaced. In this case, God decided to act on His own accord in choosing an apostle.

The word spread quickly about Paul. I think any of us would struggle trying to accept the conversion experience of someone who once killed Christians. There have been many attempts to destroy the plan of God for mankind. The persecution and elimination of God's people has been the plan of the enemy since before the fall. God reaches down into human history to make sure His will is accomplished. A heart transplant from stony to sensitive, is an operation that needs God to be the one holding the scalpel.

REFLECTION:

August 2

"When they heard all he was doing, many people came to him from Judea, Jerusalem, Idumea, and the regions across the Jordan and around Tyre and Sidon." (Mark 3:8 New International Version)

Wouldn't it be wonderful if people still gathered in our churches because they heard what Jesus was doing? Wouldn't it be wonderful if people gathered at your house because they heard what Jesus was doing? So many times, people come to hear a preacher or hear a teacher. I'm not saying there's anything wrong with that, but we are supposed to make Jesus attractive, not make some religious icon famous. I happen to believe Jesus still wants to open blind eyes, strengthen crippled legs, and give the riches of the gospel to the poor. We have considered miracles a thing of the past only to be experienced by the apostles. Maybe God isn't moving the same way because He can't find anyone willing to walk with Him the same way. We're very quick to say that God is no respecter of persons, but we excuse ourselves with average exploits.

Fasting is at best an annual event instead of a regular denial of the flesh. If you look at the book of Matthew, fasting is assumed the same way giving and praying is assumed.

REFLECTION:

August 3

"Heaven is my throne, and earth is my footstool: what house will ye build me? saith the Lord: or what is the place of my rest?" (Isaiah 66:1 King James Version).

The universe can't contain God, yet He has chosen to be local, dwelling within you! It is an amazing concept that God subjects Himself to space and time in order to relate to us. He didn't need us; we needed Him. The God that is everywhere is still personal. The temple He dwells in now is your body. The glory of God must still be seen in the temple. God wants to "rest" in your heart. He doesn't have a relationship with heaven or earth; His concern is YOU! Heaven and earth will pass away. You are ETERNAL.

REFLECTION:

August 4

"Wasn't it necessary for me, even on the Sabbath day, to free this dear woman from the bondage in which Satan has held her for eighteen years?" (Luke 13:16 New Living Translation).

When I see passages of scripture like this one, it helps me understand how ridiculous church people appear to unbelievers. God's people can get so entangled in rules and regulations that we forget PEOPLE! It isn't considered a religious "service" to deny someone wholeness because of a law. Jesus rebuked them for taking their animals for feeding and watering on the Sabbath day, yet they didn't want this woman helped. Our sacrifices only score points with God when people are edified by them. If this woman's healing had benefited the religious rulers, I'm sure they would have been in favor of it.

We are living in a time when some people care more about pets than children. We do more to protect beasts than we do to protect babies. I'm not against loving animals as I love them, too. However, we certainly must have our priorities in order. This woman was in demonic bondage and spiritual imprisonment for eighteen years. Surely her relief would be more important than what day of the week it is. God didn't establish laws for us to be bound. He established them so we could realize our own powerlessness and cry out to Him for His salvation. Unbelievers won't be convinced that we have the answers until we stop condemning each other. Like the word says, "They will know we are Christians by our love for one another."

REFLECTION:

August 5

"Do not sacrifice to the Lord your God an ox or a sheep that has any defect or flaw in it, for that would be detestable to him" (Deuteronomy 17:1 New International Version).

The first five books of the Bible contain the "law" of God. These commands weren't given to restrict God's people; on the contrary, they were given to expose the fact that we are incapable of completely living up to God's standards. It is an insult to offer God anything that He hasn't qualified. The human tendency is always to give God whatever WE want Him to have. The world's way is always about looking out for number one. I guess that would be fine if God were number one. God demands your best and will settle for nothing less After all, didn't He give you His best?

The people of God began to compromise their offerings and bring the priests defective animals. If that wasn't bad enough, the priests weren't always correcting the issue before approaching God with the sacrifice. God gives you what you need to please Him. Sometimes you have to work a little harder, but He always rewards the effort. Even today, the pick of the litter would cost you more than the run-of-the-mill pup. Trust God to help you honor Him with the best of your skills, talents, time, and treasure. When you let go of your best, He gives you back something even better.

REFLECTION:

August 6

"We have found this man to be a troublemaker, stirring up riots among the Jews all over the world. He is a ringleader of the Nazarene sect and even tried to desecrate the temple, so we seized him" (Acts 24:5 New International Version).

This is the testimony of the lawyer Tertullus. The Jews assembled another group to accuse Paul similarly to the way they conspired against Jesus. If your lifestyle resembles the one Jesus modeled, it stands to reason that you would be treated like He was. Tertullus began his case by kissing up to Felix concerning his reign of peace. One way to get someone's attention is by telling them great things about their position. Notice the constant exaggeration. If Paul was a worldwide troublemaker, Felix wouldn't have to be informed about him. The only punishment the Jewish law couldn't exact was capital punishment. Why didn't the Jewish leadership deal with their own issues short of seeking death?

The demonic influences always want your demise when you are effective against their cause. God was content to use Paul in a greater way even after his imprisonment. The consequences of living for God makes it look like you're defeated. Genuine disciples take advantage of every opportunity to glorify God, regardless of environment. Your surroundings may close in on you, but God is always closer. The only thing you should be guilty of is wreaking havoc on the kingdom of darkness.

REFLECTION:

August 7

"So Christ was once offered to bear the sins of many; and unto them that look for him shall he appear the second time without sin unto salvation" (Hebrews 9:28 King James Version).

This chapter often mentions the necessity of bloodshed in order to satisfy the priestly demands of God. There were priests and high priests who were required to sacrifice animals for the purpose of atonement. These practices were only symbolic of the satisfaction God would receive with the blood of Christ. The fact that Jesus only had to shed blood once is a staggering reality when you consider the mandates of the priesthood. Since Jesus died before the manifestation of sin, it stands to reason that God would accept Him. Jesus was proactive in His willingness to please the Father. He has the capacity to "absorb" every sin of every person ever born.

To those who have received the grace of God, there is great anticipation of His next appearance having defeated the sin He absorbed. He came the first time to reveal the plan; He will come the second time to execute it. Jesus knew the meaning and purpose behind His earthly existence. God has a plan to redeem mankind, and He needed an advocate, ambassador, and worthy sacrifice. The more we scrutinize the life of Christ, the more captivated we become. He displays the epitome of godly character and compassion. Other great leaders have displayed these attributes too, but none have the capacity within themselves to single-handedly eradicate sin. Whether He forgives it or defeats it, He has the power to subdue it.

REFLECTION:

August 8

"Therefore, what benefit were you then deriving from the things of which you are now ashamed? For the outcome of those things is death" (Romans 6:21 New American Standard).

You can spend some time in average gathering places and hear people talk about their fruitless deeds. People do things for the attention of some and the admiration of others. Paul is pointing out how the things we used to do had no value. When God took over, we should be aware of the evident change. One goal of Christianity is to look forward to the blessing of the future instead of looking back at the blight of the past. Godless behavior doesn't strengthen anyone; and it robs you of a clear conscience. The inevitable result of things that were shameful is death. Be honest and transparent as you give instructions to those following you. God wants to transform you from death before you actually die.

The majority of this sixth chapter of Romans is dedicated to the new life in Christ. You can build on what God started in you by simply yielding gratitude to Him. There are certainly tracks in our lives that we would love to erase. You can't change what was done. You can change what you're doing now, and you can be changed for the benefit of power in what you will do. Obedience affords you heaven's help to please God.

REFLECTION:

August 9

"And Jesus went about all the cities and villages, teaching in their synagogues and proclaiming the good news (the gospel) of the kingdom, and curing all kinds of disease and every weakness and infirmity" (Matthew 9:35 Amplified Bible).

The ministry of Jesus was in full swing at this point. He wanted to delegate power to His disciples after setting things straight in the halls of education. The synagogue represented the place where people expected to hear from God. It is critically important that proper teaching takes place before you hand over kingdom authority. How can you really tell if Jesus is in the vicinity? People typically look for evidence of His presence. The mark of His presence doesn't have as much to do with praise and worship as it does the simplicity of the gospel. Praise and worship are certainly an indication to the saints while deliverance is the evidence in the streets. Jesus cured diseases and rendered the powers of darkness powerless. He left nothing undetected.

We often make excuses for our weaknesses and infirmities, but He has dealt with everything. The power in the gospel is unparalleled. Sound doctrine is the foundation for any possibility of understanding kingdom principles. The ministry of Jesus was so contrary to expectation. He had to spend time giving clarity. The scriptures testify of Jesus, and Jesus glorified the Father. Don't be more concerned with being a Bible scholar than being a Christ expositor.

REFLECTION:

August 10

"Defend the cause of the weak and fatherless; maintain the rights of the poor and oppressed" (Psalms 82:3 New International Version).

This plea for justice comes from the heart of Asaph. How many times have we asked God to level the playing field for those who have been forgotten and victimized? We usually are pleading our own cause first, then MAYBE someone else's. God wants us to care about others before ourselves. What is the cause of the weak and fatherless? That "cause" consists of collective efforts to remove them from that state. The weak should be made strong, and the fatherless should be adopted. It will break your heart to see how people are treated these days.

I believe animals have more people defending them. I'm not saying animals shouldn't be defended, but we must get our priorities in order. There are many people in our world that are defenseless or weak due to some external factors. The Bible says when you lend to the poor, you lend to the Lord. The word "lend" doesn't mean to loan. It means when you extend yourself to provide what is necessary for wholeness. It's really a shame that oppression has been alive and well since the early days of human life. If every Christian lived in the center of God's will for their lives, every need would be met world-wide. The feeding of the multitudes happened because the disciples made themselves available as a channel of blessing.

REFLECTION:

August 11

"He could not do any miracles there, except lay his hands on a few sick people and heal them" (Mark 6:5 New International Version).

Be very careful how you perceive what God is doing. Jesus told the people that prophets are only dishonored in their own hometown and among their relatives. This text says He couldn't do any miracles except heal a few people. We would consider healing a great miracle. What could he have done if He had been the object of great faith? Healing isn't even considered a big deal in His economy. What have you been asking God for? What do you need more than anything else? Do you have the faith to see the possibility in Him? Do you see the probability in Him?

Don't ever ask Jesus to do something for you that you can do for yourself. God wants to equip you with the faith of Jesus! The skeptics thought they knew Him. Isn't this the carpenter's son? If you think you really know Jesus, make sure you don't restrict Him by your fears. The idea is to release Him by your faith. When you take the limits off, God can really show Himself mighty. It doesn't matter how old you are. It doesn't matter how far down the wrong road you have traveled. The only thing that matters now is whether or not you can see Him for who He really is and let Him do what He can really do.

REFLECTION:

August 12

"Has not my hand made all these things, and so they came into being? This is the one I esteem: he who is humble and contrite in spirit, and trembles at my word" (Isaiah 66:2 New International Version).

Even in the midst of vindication and incredible expressions of judgment and divine retribution; God still remembers mercy. He never forgets that He has always placed a remnant in the midst. What kind of person is God looking for? A contrite spirit doesn't wait to be confronted by man about his error. When YOU know you're wrong, conviction makes you contrite because you are actually ALWAYS caught. The things people claw, scrape, and kill to receive, God has control over. He says, "I have made these things."

Why is it harder to wait for God to give something than it is to just take it? A humble person will wait for a gift to be given instead of seeking an opportunity for a prize to be stolen. Those who tremble at the word of God are those who don't decide what to do until they know what God says. We Christians claim to be all of these things, but if we are, why are so many other religions increasing in number? God keeps a remnant to change evil environments. In order to be light and salt, we must lead and not follow. God knows who you are, what you can do, where you can go, and who you can influence. I hope your goal in life is to be one who God esteems.

REFLECTION:

August 13

"Now I will sing out my thanks to the Lord! Praise the Lord! For though I was poor and needy, he delivered me from my oppressors" (Jeremiah 20:13 New Living Translation).

There were many times in the Bible when Jesus told people not to mention their blessings publicly. Jesus never really wanted to draw attention to Himself until He was on the cross drawing the attention of all mankind. This chapter of Jeremiah is very interesting because he was enduring persecution and turned his attention to God in the midst of his trials. Jesus chose to remain inconspicuous while God wanted His works published. Even in the days of Moses and Joshua, God commanded that His goodness be spoken openly. He didn't want the next generations to forget their heritage.

Now that Christ is seated at the right hand of God, we should resume sharing His goodness. The book of Titus tells us to acknowledge the truth. It's impossible to praise silently. You can worship God silently. You can admire God silently. You can reflect on His majesty silently, but you CAN'T praise Him silently! He had mercy on you when others completely disregarded you. He equipped you when others considered you unqualified. God has great plans for the poor and needy. Why should you think your oppressors have the final say in your destiny?

REFLECTION:

August 14

"Just as Sodom and Gomorrah and the cities around them, since they in the same way as these indulged in gross immorality and went after strange flesh, are exhibited as an example, in undergoing the punishment of eternal fire" (Jude v7 New American Standard).

Every now and then we need an earth shattering, sobering reminder of God's intolerance for sin. The part of this verse I want to focus on is the part that talks about these cities being an EXAMPLE. Look at the bright side. God lets us know what not to do. Even though these cities were destroyed, God showed tremendous longsuffering. Abraham interceded for the inhabitants and bargained God all the way down to ten righteous citizens. If Abraham could find ten righteous people, God would have spared all others for the sake of the ten.

When you look at the size of your town, imagine the wicked rampage if there aren't at least ten decent people. We often wonder why God doesn't take vengeance faster than He does. If God had no patience, who would have time to make changes? The example of destruction should also help us appreciate the mercy we receive even on our so-called "good days." We should make sure we keep company with those who help us reach our goals. God doesn't want anyone to suffer or experience His wrath. He has done everything He can to help you avoid the consequences of bad choices.

The question is, "Where will I spend eternity?"

The answer is, "Wherever you want to!"

REFLECTION:

August 15

"Then he touched their eyes and said, 'According to your faith will it be done to you'" (Matthew 9:29 New International Version).

The fame of Jesus was spreading throughout the region because of the miracles he performed. The dead were raised, the sick were healed, the infirm were restored, and the blind received their sight. If you believe Jesus can fix your problem, you meet the minimum requirements for the miraculous. He didn't just "do" things because it would make Him popular. Your faith qualifies you to approach Him. Your issues, whatever they are, require His "touch" also.

I find it interesting that there is always a spiritual solution to any natural problem. Many of the Jews in Jesus' day believed that blindness and other handicaps were the result of a person's sin. Jesus often corrected those opinions because the glory of God was at work. If you are in a certain condition so the glory of God can be revealed, then you must appeal to Him. Don't assume the glory of God means you will be healed. The glory of God could simply mean that He will give you the grace to endure your condition. Whatever the case, you will have the peace of knowing He is in control. Trust Him to do the best thing for you, even though it might not be what you expected Him to do.

REFLECTION:

August 16

"Against you, and you alone, have I sinned; I have done what is evil in your sight. You will be proved right in what you say, and your judgment against me is just" (Psalms 51:4 New Living Translation).

I will add this to the list of things I admire about David: his ability to accept the consequences for his actions and seek God's forgiveness. I saw a commercial recently where people were seated at a conference table for a business meeting. The person chairing the meeting announced how they were going to have a "blamestorming" session. I marvel at the human tendency to pretend you're not guilty because no one can prove what you did. Statements like: "You didn't see me, so I'm free to go."

David covered his tracks very thoroughly, and we do too! Nathan, the prophet, was sent to confront David about his actions. God knows everything. That's right, EVERYTHING. He even knows why we get into compromising positions. He knows the condition of your heart that led to the decisions. God forgave David even though there were consequences he suffered. God's forgiveness doesn't prevent you from reaping what you sow. God confronts each of His children by His Spirit. If you can be comfortable doing wrong, you should examine whose family you belong to. God wants to have close fellowship with you at all times. When something is in the way, He will give you the grace to deal with it before He decides to.

REFLECTION:

August 17

"Just as Jannes and Jambres opposed Moses, so these {men} also oppose the truth, men of depraved mind, rejected in regard to the faith" (II Timothy 3:8 New American Standard).

Paul was very bold when it came to identifying the enemies of the cross. In describing the environment of the last days, he drew a comparison to the experiences of Moses. There has ALWAYS been resistance to the plan of God. Great men and women of God have endured great trials of affliction from those who hate God. I don't believe I have ever actually heard anyone say they hate God, but their actions reveal a hatred for anything God favors. We are truly living in perilous times. One thing we can expect is that there will be MANY with the spirit of Jannes and Jambres. Every person attempting to advance the kingdom will have someone like them trying to destroy it.

When a person's mind is depraved, they don't feel any remorse for the harm they cause. No matter how low the moral compass goes, God will still accomplish His will in the earth. There was a time when the word of the Lord was "precious" (rare). Although the written Bible is found everywhere, two-legged bibles are still "precious". If you have a living example of someone trying to mature you in the faith, consider yourself fortunate. Paul was a rare jewel in the crown of Christianity, and God still has some servants that He is pleased with today.

REFLECTION:

August 18

"When the even was come, they brought unto him many that were possessed with devils: and he cast out the spirits with [his] word, and healed all that were sick" (Matthew 8:16 King James Version).

The religious leaders were known for teaching but never really demonstrated the power that comes from a relationship with God. Many came to Jesus at night for fear of persecution. The power of God must be manifest in your life if you expect to be effective against the real strongholds of the enemy. Too many people just want to "lecture" you into favor with God. The Spirit of the Lord gives you the power to live victoriously over the schemes of the devil. Jesus subdued the plans of devils by His WORD! If you don't know the word of God, you will be very ineffective in spiritual warfare. Although sickness isn't the plan of God, it can still be strategically used for the glory of God.

The casting out of spirits doesn't come through homiletics, hermeneutics, or even expository preaching; it comes by discernment and sensitivity to His leading. The word of God is profitable. The word gives us everything we need to negotiate a successful, God-honoring life. If the word works against the enemies of God, don't you think it will be effective in promoting the will of God? Many of us need physical healing, mental healing, emotional healing, psychological healing, and relational healing. If you think everyone else is your problem, you won't get the healing you need. Go to Jesus yourself without worrying about who else should go.

REFLECTION:

August 19

"Flee also youthful lusts: but follow righteousness, faith, charity, peace, with them that call on the Lord out of a pure heart" (II Timothy 2:22 King James Version).

When the word of God tells us to flee something, I think God expects us to FLEE! Why do so many Christians go through a mental exercise to see if God really means what He says? Is there really an alternative? Because of the enlightenment of our present age, sometimes we are tempted to see "options" in the word of God. If this was multiple choice, and each choice leads to God, I believe He would have given us each option. When God gave options to Adam and Eve, they chose the only one God didn't give them.

Paul is giving Timothy very sound advice about how to successfully navigate the Christian life. We are always following something. The list of things in this verse will give you the strength to endure. I find it interesting that we are told to follow these things with others who are following the same things. No matter how strong and powerful you think you are, you still need the strength of others. The strength in the multitude will help fortify weaknesses in your character that you may not be aware of. Since Timothy was to function in leadership, he really needed to listen to his mentor. God will always provide someone you should listen to. Are you willing to let God teach you through others? Sometimes it will be someone younger with less education and less credentials. Don't worry though; God makes up the difference.

REFLECTION:

August 20

"I am your servant; give me understanding—discernment and comprehension—that I may know (discern and be familiar with the character of) Your testimonies" (Psalms 119:125 Amplified Bible).

The psalmist has made a determination that everything he needs MUST come from God. Latter Day Saints have all too often compromised their ethics, thinking goodness has many sources. If you ever expect to get understanding, it will come from God. Your spiritual wisdom and understanding will come from God. Your discerning of spirits and ranking of principalities will come from God. Your boldness to confront the darkness you encounter will come from God. Your tenacity to hold on to the word of God will come from God. The comprehension of spiritual truth, rightly dividing the word, and application of revelation will come from God.

Continue to pray that God gives you the things you need. Our God is a God of character. If things happen that confuse you, give God the benefit of the doubt. Jesus died to give you the privilege of serving God and knowing God. Do you REALLY know God? He has told us that His ways and His thoughts are not like ours. Your life is a continuing tapestry of God's creativity. The mastery of creativity lies in the power of creative influence. Let God infiltrate your life with His ingenuity. The success of your walk is dependent on someone who has been where you're going. Jesus has already felt everything coming your way.

REFLECTION:

August 21

"And God blessed the seventh day and sanctified it: because that in it he had rested from all his work which God created and made" (Genesis 2:3 King James Version).

God didn't rest because He was tired, so we might look at this as God stopped working and set aside a special day. Everything else in God's creative mind was spoken into existence when God said, "Let there be." However, when it came to man, God both created AND made him. So, God wanted man to be a unique creation. He said, "Let us make man in our image and after our likeness." You are the image of God, and you represent what God delights in. After He spoke His mind concerning man's creation, He shaped him from the ground and breathed life into his nostrils. That first divine exhale is where your creativity, imagination, and vision came from. Even after the fall, we still have the privilege of these benefits.

We must make sure that God receives the fruit from what He gives us. I believe God rested so He could admire His creation. I also believe He wanted to enjoy fellowship with the universe. He created the heavens and the earth. I think we pay too much attention to the heavens, and not enough attention to the earth. Since the earth is where we reside, it would be more practical to absorb the awe of God right here. I'm afraid we often seek blessings far away and overlook the blessings right under our noses.

REFLECTION:

August 22

"For the law never made anything perfect—but instead a better hope is introduced through which we [now] come close to God" (Hebrews 7:19 Amplified Bible).

The law was designed to expose our inadequacies and make us yearn to have our internal emptiness filled. There are many who claim to have kept the law, but the same law they claim to have kept included sacrifices for transgressions. Even the priests that handled the sacrifices were commanded to atone for their own sins first, then offer sacrifice for the sins of the people. Man has the audacity to think he can hit a divine standard. Things impossible for man are ordinary for God. Your better hope has a name: JESUS! He gave us a better hope because the only way to measure up to God's standard is by total reliance upon Him.

God is holy, perfect, without flaw, and absent of defect. He is actually the standard of perfection. There is none like Him! Only God can measure up to God. The way our better hope reached us is through the avenue of love, grace, kindness, forbearance, forgiveness, and countless other covenant categories. If God didn't want a relationship with you, you wouldn't have a relationship with Him. Life would be a constant nightmare because we still wouldn't know if today would be our last. The better hope allows us to be close to God in this life and live in anticipation of His literal, visible presence in the life to come.

REFLECTION:

August 23

"For I am planting seeds of peace and prosperity among you. The grapevines will be heavy with fruit. The earth will produce its crops, and the sky will release the dew. Once more I will make the remnant in Judah and Israel the heirs of these blessings" (Zechariah 8:12 New Living Translation).

The things God plants take time to grow. You don't become a spiritual giant in a short while. There are no overnight sensations in the kingdom. As a matter of fact, the more you grow, the more you realize you're a product of God's grace. Peace and prosperity should be music to our ears. What can be more discouraging than a fruitless vine? When you see how long and hard you have worked, you certainly look forward to fruit and harvest. But sometimes God has to remind you that increase doesn't come from hard work alone. If God doesn't bless your efforts, your work is futile. But take heart, God always keeps His promises. As heirs of God and joint heirs with Jesus Christ, blessings can't miss you.

The dew from heaven is symbolic of the favor of God. He provides the moisture to your roots that allows the works of your hands to be fruitful. People today will try to make you think that God just hands out favor to everyone in His family. Well, this passage mentions a remnant. Even among the people of God, there are some that get His attention more than others. He loves us all the same, but He responds to us according to our obedience.

REFLECTION:

August 24

"Lowborn men are but a breath, the highborn are but a lie; if weighed on a balance, they are nothing; together they are only a breath" (Psalms 62:9 New International Version).

No matter what your status in life, there still remains a common need. God sees every person alike. Those born in less than enviable surroundings are here briefly. Those born in enviable surroundings think they will enjoy an extended life but are also only here briefly. When value is extracted from your life, it won't be based on what everyone else thought of you. The value of your life depends on how much interest God earns for the investment He placed in you.

The book of Romans tells us that we are altogether unprofitable. If we were to add everyone together, we wouldn't add value to heaven based on our natural state. The psalmist knew that it wouldn't benefit him to be a people pleaser. The high society elite will give you the impression that you should be like them. The reality is: to whom much is given much is required; and to whom one has committed much, of him he will ask more. Be faithful with what passes through your grasp because there is opportunity to invest it in the things of God. It is wonderful to know that God will accept your offering regardless of your social status. When you treat God properly, He can change your status.

REFLECTION:

August 25

"Now we command you, brethren, in the name of our Lord Jesus Christ, that ye withdraw yourselves from every brother that walketh disorderly, and not after the tradition which he received of us" (II Thessalonians 3:6 King James Version).

There are few believers that follow this principle. We shouldn't act self-righteous, but we certainly want to make sure we're not infected by the contrary attitude of some. Paul wanted to protect the sincere believers and ensure they continued in the growth process. To "withdraw" means to back up. We don't have to completely abandon them, but there should be enough distance for them to feel the need to change. Paul spent tremendous energy planting the word into the spirits of God's people. I'm all for restoration and encouragement, but we also have to be discerning and prayerful.

Believe it or not, some people don't really want their circumstances to change. God has made it possible for His children to benefit from His grace in ways that are life changing. The Thessalonians' church responded greatly to the gospel and their faith increased quickly. They were very involved in meeting the needs of the church. Paul knew that their heart for God could make them vulnerable to people wanting to take advantage of them. Sometimes you just have to let God have His way without your active involvement. But you CAN pray.

REFLECTION:

August 26

"But avoid stupid and foolish controversies and genealogies and dissensions and wrangling about the Law, for they are unprofitable and futile" (Titus 3:9 Amplified Bible).

If you are serving in any capacity of leadership, you should expect controversy to come looking for you. Paul is urging Titus to remember why he was left in Crete. He was to establish leaders that weren't caught up in pointless intellectual exercises. There were even those who were using the Christian faith for dishonest gain or profit. If you are going to avoid anything, you have to be aware of disguises. Many things come disguised as a prayer request, a leadership meeting, a Bible study, or a church event.

The Bible is clear that although all things are permissible; all things aren't beneficial. There will always be differences of opinion, but we don't have to enter into endless debates about them. The plan of the enemy is to get us distracted about things that have no real solution. Even if you win the argument, you probably haven't influenced the person. The church needs leaders that understand their calling, accept their assignment, and will complete their mission. There will be many things you must avoid if you plan to fight a good fight, finish your course, and keep the faith!

REFLECTION:

August 27

"When the earth totters, and all the inhabitants of it, It is I who will poise and keep steady its pillars. Selah [pause, and calmly think of that]" (Psalms 75:3 Amplified Bible).

I don't know if you've ever really stopped to notice just how volatile the earth really is. Atmospheric conditions, magnetic implications, and conditions elsewhere in our solar system are responsible for all sorts of strange occurrences. God gave dominion of the earth to Adam. I believe God wanted Adam to rule on earth while God ruled in heaven. Adam surrendered that authority to Satan, and things have been in disarray ever since. Even with hurricanes, tornadoes earthquakes, tsunamis, and every other "natural" phenomenon, God still reigns supreme. If God didn't intervene and impose His goodness, there would be constant havoc.

People often ask, "How could God let this happen?" Actually, God is preventing complete destruction by imposing His grace and mercy. God gives the earth and the earth's inhabitants, consolation and stability. Have you ever seen the pillars of the earth? God controls the invisible. He could make it seem as though the world is suspended in midair. Gravity is a force to be reckoned with, although it can't be seen. When you ponder just how awesome God is, the only fitting response is to "pause and calmly think of that!"

REFLECTION:

August 28

"For I will pour water on the thirsty land, and streams on the dry ground; I will pour out my Spirit on your offspring, and my blessing on your descendants" (Isaiah 44:3 New International Version).

God is very interested in your estate. He wants to refresh you periodically. We carry burdens and issues that cause our spirits and environments to be quite parched. Sometimes it isn't even our own circumstances that drain us. It was good for the people of God to hear this because they experienced very dry seasons. When there is a promise of water, you can plan for a harvest. If the ground isn't properly nourished, you can't plant seeds. The promise of a generational outpouring of the Spirit encourages us because we can be a light to others. Walking with God carries many benefits that are too numerous to list. The word of God is vitally encouraging when you find yourself in captivity.

The bondage of foreigners is something American Christians can't conceive. Imagine how difficult it would be to focus on God when you see nothing else favorable. We should be consistent in honoring God for His goodness. Many of us have already enjoyed more than others can even imagine. God answers prayer. God fulfills dreams. God secures destinies. God delights in relationship, and God has proven Himself many times over. The challenge comes when you don't like your current situation. Keep walking, keep pressing, and keep praying because refreshment will keep coming.

REFLECTION:

August 29

"To do what is right and just is more acceptable to the Lord than sacrifice" (Proverbs 21:3 New International Version).

God was so pleased with sacrifice that He orchestrated an entire system of how to approach Him. He separated a specific tribe of priests to handle this elaborate system of forgiveness, restoration, and atonement. The shedding of blood appeased the holy nature of God so that we could have fellowship with Him. HOWEVER, if you aren't concerned with justice, equity, and obedience, God isn't concerned with your sacrifices. He always values the person even more than the principles. There are a few instances in the bible where it appears God was extremely harsh. Whenever you see something in the word that makes you wonder about God's reasoning, you should assume there is something you don't know. God doesn't reveal to us what He sees in the hearts of those He judges.

God wants to accept you, so He gave you an opportunity for forgiveness in Christ. This is the only modern way to approach God. Even though He died about 2,000 years ago, He is still the modern way to God. He is the ONLY way to God! Doing the right thing with the right motive is more than just a notion. You need His power to do His will, in His way, by His order, and for His glory.

REFLECTION:

August 30

"Don't try to get rich by extortion or robbery. And if your wealth increases, don't make it the center of your life" (Psalms 62:10 New Living Translation).

For most or all of our life, we have been deceived about what real success is. Because most people consider success a good salary, or an enviable job, we don't always investigate the steps to perceived success. How often do you really know what you have to do once you get that all important position? The Bible tells us plainly that riches received improperly put you at odds with God. There are apparently enough earthly resources for you to climb the ladder of success without ruining others. When you live an honest life, God will bless the work of your hands. Even if you get rich the right way, make sure you don't become confident in your wealth.

Do you know people who have money as the center of their life? Most of us would answer no. God won't share His glory with anything or anyone. When you make something else the center of your life, you're saying that God isn't worthy of that honorable position. Everything you have comes from Him, even when you disobey Him to get it! Life lessons come from choices that lead to other choices. You can either sink deeper into trouble, or you can take heed to good counsel. Don't be an example. Be a testimony.

REFLECTION:

August 31

"So, the people could not distinguish the shout of joy from the sound of the weeping of the people, for the people shouted with a loud shout, and the sound was heard far off" (Ezra 3:13 Amplified Bible).

This verse generates mixed emotions and perspectives from many of God's people. So, let me give you mine. I think there is great benefit from knowing how God wonderfully blessed in the past. However, I don't think those who have walked with God for many years and seen Him do many mighty works should stifle the joy of those who are in the realm of divine discovery. God is still worthy of praise for His acts, even when you decide that it doesn't compare to what He did yesterday. The Bible tells us to rejoice with those who rejoice. The mature Christians should be the best examples of this.

When a child discovers that a magnet can move a nail before touching it, would you tarnish their joy because you've seen better? I certainly hope not. Always remember that God isn't obligated to impress you. He's obligated to express His love to His children. Just the fact that God gave His people the strength, togetherness, and fortitude to rebuild, should have been cause to celebrate. Everything God does is spectacular. Don't ever let ANYONE'S unwillingness to participate in your victory diminish your perception of God's magnitude. What He's doing for you is a big deal because He's doing it for you. Be thankful for His desire to bless you.

REFLECTION:

SEPTEMBER

September 1

"She named the boy Ichabod, saying, "The glory has departed from Israel: because of the capture of the ark of God and the deaths of her father-in-law and her husband" (I Samuel 4:21 New International Version).

This is a very low point in the history of God's people. The wife of Phinehas wasn't even named here. Phinehas was a son of Eli the priest. Even though Eli was extremely instrumental in the guiding of Samuel, he wasn't a very good father. God was angry with Eli because he allowed his two sons, Hophni and Phinehas, to operate in the priesthood without discipline. This unbridled corruption led to the capture of the Ark of the Covenant and also to the untimely deaths of Eli and both his sons. God has a way of chastising His leaders and still causing His will to prevail.

The current leadership had to make way for Samuel because God was about to use him mightily. Don't be discouraged when you see things in terrible shape. Even though "the glory had departed" from God's people, Christ in you is the hope of glory. God was in the midst of judgment and still had a plan to deliver His people. We must stay prayerful in order that the heavy hand of God won't fall in our generation. There are many things happening that could cause the anger of God to kindle. Yet, the sacrifice of Jesus satisfied the holy indignation God had with mankind. We really don't know just how sufficient Jesus is!

REFLECTION:

September 2

"Remember those who led you, who spoke the word of God to you; and considering the result of their conduct, imitate their faith" (Hebrews 13:7 New American Standard).

Do you know anyone that gives you the word of God to pattern your life after? Has God anointed anyone in your life with scriptural insight? The answer to both questions is an emphatic, "YES!" Now, here's another question: why don't you do anything they say? People read God's word, hear God's word, are placed under the authority of gifted leadership, and still go away and do whatever feels good. Even worse, they wonder why their life is a fiasco. God says, "If you sew to your flesh, you will reap corruption." I don't think we believe that will happen every time.

Find someone in your life whose faith you can imitate and DO it. When your turn comes to answer to God, He won't care about the circumstances of your life. Jesus died for every circumstance. Therefore, even a slave won't be able to justify their rebellion. God says He has given you everything you need in order to respond like His child. He made you and bought you, so there's no excuse He will listen to. Oops, I forgot, there is ONE excuse He will listen to. If you can convince Him that your life was worse than the humiliation of the cross Jesus was nailed to, then He will accept that. That would also mean that the death of Christ was inadequate to deal with your dilemmas. Good luck with that one.

REFLECTION:

September 3

"For let him who wants to enjoy life and see good days (good whether apparent or not), keep his tongue free from evil, and his lips from guile (treachery, deceit)" (I Peter 3:10 Amplified Bible).

God desires that we have the best of everything. The thing is, we can only expect good to come if we conduct ourselves according to His guidelines. When you do things God's way, you see the good even when it's not on the surface. God knows how to give you insight and vision into His pleasure. The only ones who have His vantage point are the ones that He takes pleasure in. Position yourself to receive what He has in store for you. Peter learned how to accept the will of God even when things weren't easy. The Bible said that Job was able to prevent from sinning with his mouth or charging God foolishly.

Sometimes we think we can tell how God feels based on what is happening in our lives or the life of another. Keep your words about God pure and your words about others innocent. One thing God doesn't like is slander. Do you want to enjoy life? Do you want the blessing of God's favor? Do you see yourself concerned with God's wishes? If your answers to those questions are all yes, you would do well to follow Peter's advice. Make up your mind that you will listen to sound advice, rather than having to learn everything from experience.

REFLECTION:

September 4

"They answered him, 'We are Abraham's descendants and have never been slaves of anyone. How can you say that we shall be set free?'" (John 8:33 New International Version).

Your spiritual life is completely different than your natural life, yet because the two constantly merge, you think they coexist in harmony. Your two natures coexist in constant conflict. The battles between good and evil, God and Satan, and flesh and spirit are ALWAYS raging. The freedom Jesus offered in this chapter had to do with being able to please God. The answer these Jews gave Jesus concerning their ancestry shows they had forgotten their heritage. Moses was raised up to lead the children of Israel out of bondage. Just because some good things happen in your life doesn't mean you have never been in bondage.

The book of Romans makes it clear that liberty came through Isaac, even though faith came through Abraham. Jesus is attempting to address the ownership that sin takes in your life. Things become so "natural" that it doesn't seem to be an enemy to you. Seducing spirits harm you without hurting you. We tend to associate pain with danger, so we usually can't detect the poison mixed with the sugar. We live in a society that thanks God for nothing and blames God for everything. He knows how to lead you to freedom if you really want to go. Here again, we see the only thing worse than having a great need is thinking you need nothing.

REFLECTION:

September 5

"Then the Spirit lifted me up, and I heard behind me a loud rumbling sound—May the glory of the Lord be praised in his dwelling place" (Ezekiel 3:12 New International Version).

For the job Ezekiel had facing him, he REALLY needed to be lifted by the Spirit and in his spirit. God's prophets weren't soft-hearted or soft-spoken. The word of the Lord carried tremendous burdens and required absolute courage. If you aren't empowered by the Spirit, don't expect to have any lasting influence. The sound from behind tells you that power is behind you and God has your back. Your confidence must be in the glory of the Lord. We never know what circumstances will exhibit God's glory. You can't judge by your feelings, nor your experiences, nor anyone's counsel. You need to rely completely on the peace of God ruling your heart. Trying to do a "trip-tik" with God will land you in a world of frustration. God always leads; you always follow. The dwelling place of the Lord is everywhere He is worshiped and adored. God's glory will shine brightly when you can find the ability to worship through concern, fear, anxiety, doubt, and despair. As humans, we will experience every emotion in the "rainbow," but we don't have to be controlled by any of them.

REFLECTION:

September 6

"See what [an incredible] quality of love the Father has given (shown, bestowed on) us, that we should [be permitted to] be named and called and counted the children of God! And so we are! The reason that the world does not know (recognize, acknowledge) us, is that it does not know (recognize, acknowledge) Him" (I John 3:1 Amplified Bible).

Pull over from your hectic break-neck world and take the time to digest what God has given you! We often spend far too much time chasing what we don't have and devaluing what we do have. God has manifested His love toward us in incredible ways so we can confidently move through life. There isn't a moment where He stops declaring His love for you. It's one thing to have feelings; and another thing entirely to declare those feelings by what you do.

You are a child of God! Is there any higher privilege? Is there any greater heritage? Can you receive a more noble inheritance? Don't be dismayed because the world rejects you. The world is supposed to be estranged to its foreigners. You are a citizen of another country. Expect to receive similar treatment to Christ's. He still intends to bless you in front of your enemies. He took the pain out of your gain. Quality defines what you get from God because infinity defines Who it comes from. Actually, infinity is still inadequate to define who it comes from.

REFLECTION:

September 7

"Their leader will be one of their own; their ruler will arise from among them. I will bring him near and he will come close to me, for who is he who will devote himself to be close to me?" (Jeremiah 30:21 New International Version).

This may not sound like much to you, but it was music to the ears of these oppressed people. God told His prophet to announce an extended period of captivity to His people. This was to be a time of great anguish and turmoil under the hand of the Babylonians. This prophecy is what Daniel was reading when he didn't understand why things didn't change after 70 years of captivity. However, God was talking about a completely different make-up of 70 years. Anyway, the point of this reference is to let the people know that God plans to release them from their captors and bring authority from within. It gives much more security to a group when they know their leader.

When a foreigner rules over you, there is always the fear that your people will be abused and treated with scorn. God often used cruel dictators to punish His people for their constant rebellion against Him. God told His people that He will raise up a ruler that will be close to Him, one the people can trust to live out godly principles, and one whose sole purpose would be to draw close to Him. There was only One who fulfilled that prophecy!

REFLECTION:

September 8

"Through You we will push back our adversaries; through Your name we will trample down those who rise up against us" (Psalms 44:5 New American Standard).

Enemies must be pushed down because they always rise. You can't really predict what direction they will come from, but you have to be ready to engage them. Another thing you should be aware of is that enemies also rise from within. Your mind tries to focus on things familiar to it. Don't ever say, "I would never do that!" Conditions unfamiliar to you can cause unbelievable actions in you. The Bible tells us not to have confidence in the flesh. The psalmist was careful to give God credit for things that haven't happened yet. God empowered you to defeat yesterday's enemies. God equips you to defeat today's enemies, and He encourages you to defeat tomorrow's enemies, too. The name of the Lord has more authority than any other authoritative force. When the name is properly used, there is nothing that can stand against you. When you trample something, it doesn't even hinder your progress. Imagine being so focused on the will of God that your enemies are just mowed over without even slowing your momentum! There will always be something resisting you, either internally or externally. Feed and fortify your spirit by feeding on the word of God. When your life is characterized by these victories, others new to the faith will draw strength from your example.

REFLECTION:

_____

_____

_____

_____

_____

_____

_____

_____

September 9

"For as many as are of the works of the law are under the curse: for it is written, Cursed is every one that continueth not in all things which are written in the book of the law to do them" (Galatians 3:10 King James Version).

If your focus is on your achievement, you're missing the boat. Even as believers, we must accept the reality that God works in us to will and to do of His good pleasure. Your submission to God doesn't help your position; it helps your CONDITION! You would have to keep the whole law of God perfectly in order for Him to accept you apart from Jesus. There are crowns mentioned in scripture, but I have yet to see a crown of achievement. Jesus freed you from the demands of the law to live in the power of grace. If Jesus didn't live through you, there would be nothing about your life that impresses God. Do your best but understand that your best is still filthy rags compared to the righteousness of God. Thanks be to God for the miracle of salvation.

REFLECTION:

September 10

"Proud men have hidden a snare for me; they have spread out the cords of their net and have set traps for me along my path" (Psalms 140:5 New International Version).

Whenever you make progress, it seems there is an obstacle waiting in the same progressive path. What is it about life that challenges your determination? Your enemies spend entirely too much time trying to figure out how to stop you! If they spent just half that amount of time ordering their own lives, they would see how good God could be to them too. It takes time, wisdom, talent, creativity, and ingenuity to "design" a trap. The psalmist knew who his adversaries were. We get into trouble thinking we know who is for us and who is against us. The psalms are filled with the thrill of victory and the agony of defeat. Don't allow your faith to ride the same roller coaster as your emotions. Don't allow your hope to be darkened by dark circumstances. God knows how much you can handle, and He will handle everything else. There will be many snares, dangers, nets, traps, and ambushes, yet this is on YOUR path. Whatever you face on your path is designed to strengthen you. The proud in heart have a lofty estimate of themselves. Well, just like any other "estimate," the truth is much different. God already sees you on the other side of your path. This body will eventually wear out. Does your soul and spirit have to wear out, too?

REFLECTION:

September 11

"And the Lord their God will save them in that day as the flock of His people; for they are as the stones of a crown, sparkling in His land" (Zechariah 9:16 New American Standard).

God often speaks of how He plans to use His people. There are many innovative ways God will make you the envy of His enemies. Since His enemies are your enemies, expect Him to establish you as His crowning achievement. He won't forget any of you. His flock will be delivered in its entirety. He speaks of His heritage as one flock and not a collection of individuals. It would be a shame to have a crown with missing jewels. This chapter of Zechariah also shows how God uses His people as a bow in His hand. Victory is assured whether you are an instrument in His hands or a spectator through His defense.

Sometimes God will just have you stand still and witness His destructive prowess. The result God is looking for is that the world will know that He rules in heaven and earth. Every knee will bow, and every tongue shall confess that Jesus is Lord, thereby glorifying God. Prepare yourself and be strong in the Lord. The sparkle of your character will be the essence of His glory. God loves to show you off. Stay close to Him and expect to be constantly on His mind and within His reach.

REFLECTION:

September 12

"Do not be deceived and deluded and misled; God will not allow Himself to be sneered at—scorned, disdained or mocked [by mere pretensions or professions, or His precepts being set aside]—He inevitably deludes himself who attempts to delude God. For whatever a man sows, that and that only is what he will reap" (Galatians 6:7 Amplified Bible).

Very few professionals will tell you that one cause of depression could be that you can't handle getting back what you've given out. This verse is commonly used to straighten out other people. I have never heard it used as a verse for self-examination. Actually, God gives His entire word for self-examination. In light of this revelation, can anyone say to God, "But this isn't fair?" I'll let you answer that question for yourself. Many of us have no problem accepting the credit for the good things in life. I'm certainly not suggesting that handicaps and things of that nature are a result of what we did. Those things are a result of Adam's sin.

Reaping from your life is a result of your own sins and not the sin of mankind. However, we should also be willing to accept the responsibility for some of the "bad" things in life. The point is: God refuses to put Himself in a position where He has to explain Himself. God is above reproach, yet He is not beyond approach. The Bible explains life, reduces life to acceptable terms, and even predicts outcomes for us. God has done all that He intends to do for us to have the abundant life. He has tried to eliminate many of life's surprises. If you seldom dialogue with Him through His word, expect to be constantly surprised.

REFLECTION:

September 13

"Though you grind a fool in a mortar, grinding him like grain with a pestle, you will not remove his folly from him" (Proverbs 27:22 New International Version).

This is a very graphic depiction of human nature. It seems like this would be a pretty hopeless case. This verse is just trying to tell that: folly cannot be dealt with by punishment, but it can be minimized by instruction. And with issues concerning the nature of a person, you can't defeat it with an external force, so you must bring about an internal change. The wisdom of Solomon reveals the goals of God. Jesus also understood what God intended to accomplish and set His sights on teaching and preaching, giving us the necessary tools to live out salvation. We are told that the rod of correction drives foolishness out of the heart of a child. Children don't have the wisdom to make profitable decisions, so correction helps them understand on their level. God spends our entire lifetime trying to get instruction to us. He speaks through nature. He speaks through trials. He speaks through His word, and He speaks to our minds. He only resorts to punishment when we have constantly disregarded His call or when we are bent on destruction.

REFLECTION:

September 14

"I will betroth you to me forever; I will betroth you in righteousness and justice, in love and compassion" (Hosea 2:19 New International Version).

Hosea had the unenviable distinction of really knowing the pains of infidelity. He was actually married to a prostitute at the request of God. It's hard to imagine the agony of knowing you don't have a special place in the life of the one you're in covenant with. God's heart was aching because He wasn't "special" in the hearts and lives of His people. However, God clarified His commitment to them despite their indiscretions. God believed He could "out love" their faithlessness. It seems as though God understands how difficult it is to stand under His chastisement.

Although God gets angry, He doesn't lose His compassion. Every time His children cried out for relief from their oppressors, He delivered them. We often suffer the consequences of our own decisions, but God still finds a way to reach us. A betrothal is the same as a marriage in the eyes of God. The betrothal period is like an engagement. There is one difference. An engagement allows you to get the care of your beloved while you keep the security of your parents. God takes care of us like a divine husband even though we are still in our current human state. In our case, it will still be MUCH better when we enjoy the provision of God fully in His kingdom.

REFLECTION:

September 15

"For we are each responsible for our own conduct" (Galatians 6:5 New Living Translation).

I think many thousands of people have forgotten this verse is still in the Bible. I looked up the word "blame" in the scriptures, and I was surprised to discover that it always dealt with perception, not reality. The only exception was in the book of Ephesians when it declares us to be holy and without blame before God. Every other occurrence had to do with how a person appeared to another person. God doesn't allow us to blame anyone else for our conduct. Unfortunately, that doesn't stop blame from becoming an epidemic of excuses. Races blame other races. Denominations blame other denominations. Spouses blame each other. Children blame teachers. The poor blame the rich, and so on, and so on. To add to this dilemma, verse two in this same chapter tells us to bear one another's burdens. When it comes to helping restore someone, we should help them carry their load. When it comes to helping ourselves, we must watch our motives. I must admit there are compensating factors, extenuating circumstances, and environmental influences, but God still holds us accountable to His word! Jesus defeated every evil you can possibly face in order that you wouldn't be defeated. God gave you the authority to function in every area of responsibility. It would be unfair of Him to give you an order you can't follow.

REFLECTION:

September 16

"But Naaman became angry and stalked away. 'I thought he would surely come out to meet me,' he said. 'I expected him to wave his hand over the leprosy and call on the name of the Lord his God and heal me'" (II Kings 5:11 New Living Translation).

What do you want the Lord to do for you? If the will of God is in your favor and you want the same thing He wants for you, why don't you have it? We should ask ourselves these searching questions from time to time. Naaman was a mighty man under the king of Aram. He was a skilled warrior, and God used him to bring many victories. But, Naaman had leprosy. I have a suspicion that Naaman's issue was conceit, even more than his leprosy. He thought he was too important to wash in the Jordan and obey the word of the Lord. How many times have you already decided how God should bless you? What right do we have to "expect" God to use our methods to deliver His blessings?

Arrogance in a sinful state can certainly prevent God from blessing us. Let's go back to the first question. If you don't have something God wants you to have, it is probably because you won't do what He said in order to receive it. You ALWAYS have a participatory role in whatever you want God to do. You can't force God to bless you while you continue to be president of your own life. Ask the Lord what He wants FROM you in order to receive what He has FOR you. Our sinful state makes leprosy look like a walk in the park. God really wants to bless you. Do you want to be blessed? Follow His rules.

REFLECTION:

September 17

"In a moment, in the twinkling of an eye, at the last trump: for the trumpet shall sound, and the dead shall be raised incorruptible, and we shall be changed" (I Corinthians 15:52 King James Version).

The ninth chapter of Hebrews talks heavily about the necessity of death as the vehicle to bring a new testament. In the case of Jesus, this is a much better testament. The plan of God was to apprehend those who would receive Him. We must have our sins dealt with if we expect to have a relationship with God. You couldn't deal with your own sin in a satisfactory manner. God needed to abolish them, not just hide or cover them. If Jesus bore your sins, you should be looking for Him. When He shows up the next time, He won't still be carrying the sins He carried away. When He returns, He will consummate the final chapter of your salvation experience. He has justified you in spite of your past, sanctified you for His present purpose, and upon His return He will glorify you for His future enjoyment.

The book of Hebrews te s us how much better Jesus is. The death of Jesus was an offering for the sins of the entire world. Although the entire world won't be saved, there is room for the world in the will of God. The atoning, sacrificial death of Christ allows for the vilest person to be saved. He offered Himself willingly to the praise of God's glory. If He had not given Himself, we would have no possibility of eternal life.

REFLECTION:

_____

_____

_____

_____

_____

_____

_____

_____

September 18

"For I am the least of the apostles and do not even deserve to be called an apostle, because I persecuted the church of God" (I Corinthians 15:9 New International Version).

Paul never forgot how much God's grace afforded him. When you look at the far-reaching impact Paul's ministry had, you would think that he was probably the greatest apostle. I guess we should measure ourselves according to the goal, even if others measure us according to history's impact. Paul functioned out of religious zeal when he was destroying the church. God knew He wouldn't have to worry about Paul ever taking credit for the fruit of his life. I heard a man recently say, "Can you imagine how much we could accomplish if nobody cared who gets the credit?"

If our passion resulted in God getting the glory, I believe we could change the world! Sometimes we do more damage to the body of Christ after our conversion. Paul also mentioned how God had mercy on him because he did his damage in ignorance. Trust the Lord to choose His own soldiers. We can't see anyone's heart. The change in Paul's life was thorough, genuine, and persuasive. He also mentioned how his lifestyle matched his preaching. How you see yourself determines how much you actually change. See yourself as one who has received tremendous grace, so you never have to trip over your ego.

REFLECTION:

September 19

"Be anxious for nothing, but in everything by prayer and supplication with thanksgiving, let your requests be made known to God" (Philippians 4:6 New American Standard).

Life coming at you with perilous speed can cause great anxiety. God still wants His children to know that He is in charge and in complete control. He can give your heart relief without giving you an explanation. Even if He explained His plan to you in detail, you still wouldn't be able to comprehend how everything connects together. Commit the most important aspects of your concerns to prayer. He will give you direction and guidance. Don't forget to be thankful because things could be a lot worse. Don't forget to be thankful because God can make any decision He pleases. Expressing thanks before making your request shows that you know your concern is in the proper hands.

God won't always make decisions that will bring you security. However, He will ALWAYS make decisions for your good and His glory. Peter tells us to cast all of our cares on Him because He cares for you. The next verse in this chapter promises us His peace that passes all understanding. So, it isn't important for you to have an understanding. It is of paramount importance that you have confidence in His love and dependence on His grace and mercy.

REFLECTION:

September 20

"Those who err in spirit will come to understanding, and those who murmur [discontentedly] will accept instruction" (Isaiah 29:34 Amplified Bible).

The stress of everyday life can sometimes have you feeling like things will never change. When you do something long enough to form a habit, how can it be broken? The course of the world doesn't change the plan of God. The course of your mind doesn't change the plan of God. The determined council of God has already said what shall be. Our goal should be to position ourselves in the greatest possible vantage point to maximize His plan. Understanding is insight into realms previously mysterious to you. God wants you to know as much as you can handle. When you have reached a limit, you can share with someone else, allowing Him to pour into you again. Even those who murmur are convinced to receive instruction. Have you ever heard of a life expert? God will cause and allow things in your life that only one book can address. God used many authors to bring His word to completion. You can't afford to be discontent because you don't know everything. The hidden things belong to the ones who get close enough to the whisper. The events in your life will draw you or drive you.

REFLECTION:

September 21

"Whoever tends the fig tree shall eat the fruit of it, so he who patiently and faithfully guards and heeds his master shall be honored" (Proverbs 27:18 New International Version).

It stands to reason that those who invest in the growth and development of others should be refreshed by the fruit of their labors. Many people will try to treat you as though you should just give your pearls with no benefit. Ask the Lord to lead you as it relates to where He wants you to labor. You have a Master in heaven, so don't think there isn't any accountability for your gifts. Solomon gives us principles for life and rules for stewardship. Biblical leadership was constantly concerned about who wanted to take over for them. Everyone wasn't content with waiting their turn to ascend the throne. It would be wonderful if people would take advice from the current ruler and use that to establish their own rule. You can see here that God designed His system so that the laborers were the beneficiaries.

The people of God must be determined to roll up their sleeves, turn over the soil, and wait for God to nurture His people. Your master is whoever you decide to yield allegiance to. God wants to honor your faithfulness, diligence, and commitment. You don't have to be someone special, just someone yielded. In the Old Testament, the fig tree was symbolic of the nation of Israel. When you are patient, faithful, and obedient, you can expect God to move on your behalf.

REFLECTION:

September 22

"The next morning the Jews formed a conspiracy and bound themselves with an oath not to eat or drink until they had killed Paul" (Acts 23:12 New International Version).

This plot of the Jews came right after an appearance of the Lord to Paul where He explained how Paul would have to testify in Rome. The following chapters talk about how years passed, and Paul was still alive. Sometimes religious acts can be insane. I don't think the Jewish leaders were able to fulfill that oath. When God shows you favor, others who claim to be servants of God can cause the greatest resistance. God has a job for you to do, which means you can't be stopped unless He stops you. Find out what God expects you to accomplish and make sure you're doing it. You have been equipped for the times you are living in. This particular plot had more than forty men involved. Paul was told about the plot and knew that God was still going to use him. Paul was told to "take courage."

Your assignment won't necessarily be an easy one. Anytime someone vows to God in order to eliminate you, deep hatred is obvious. This kind of hatred is demonic, so you will need to walk closely with God so you don't lose your mind. God knows how to prepare you for the things coming your way. Short-term plots never outdo long-term plans.

REFLECTION:

September 23

"He has remembered his love and his faithfulness to the house of Israel; all the ends of the earth have seen the salvation of our God" (Psalms 98:3 New International Version).

Aren't you glad God doesn't treat you according to your weaknesses and your actions? God delights in showing mercy. He even wants to be merciful to your enemies. The people of Israel have always had God on their side. He wants to use them as a light to other nations. God still wants to use His people today to be a light to the world. The faithfulness of God causes Him to act according to His covenant. Even when we deny Him, the Bible teaches that He cannot deny Himself. The world has had the opportunity to witness the goodness of God offered in salvation. How can the love of God be adequately defined? The word of God tells us that His love passes knowledge. His love is immeasurable. His love is unquenchable. He is determined to love you and find many ways to reveal love to you.

Life's circumstances and hardships aren't indicative of His love toward you. We have made many mistakes, bad decisions, and even pre-meditated actions that have ruined opportunities in the natural. In the spiritual, there is nothing you could do to disqualify yourself as a recipient of His love and attention.

REFLECTION:

September 24

"In your unfailing love, silence my enemies; destroy all my foes, for I am your servant" (Psalms 143:12 New International Version).

There are many pertinent ingredients of prayer. First, focus on God's love for you. Even when you don't exactly pray in the will of God, He understands your heart. There is nothing wrong with asking God to deal with your enemies. After all, He plans to handle them anyway. Be careful not to request carnal antidotes for spiritual problems. There will always be a measure of resistance to the things He has called you to accomplish. God wants the things hindering you to one day establish you. He will build endurance in you without destroying you. He will build character in you without totally discouraging you. He will overshadow you with His presence when the time is right. Because you are His servant, He will treat you like His friend. First Corinthians 13 tells us that love never fails. It doesn't matter how much faith you have, and it doesn't require fervent hope.

Your success is founded in love, grounded in love, and bound in love. He died for you as man, and He lives for you as God. Don't forget all the plans He has for you. Your plans sometimes need amending, but His plans NEVER fail!

REFLECTION:

September 25

"Therefore, since we have so great a cloud of witnesses surrounding us, let us also lay aside every encumbrance and the sin which so easily entangles us, and let us run with endurance the race that is set before us" (Hebrews 12:1 New American Standard)

There are countless sympathizers watching us. I know you feel as though you are the only one dealing with a situation like yours. We have many trailblazers who can relate. Not only can they relate, but they can also "coach" you by their example. Furthermore, they can testify of God's faithfulness and dependability. A witness recounts events that determine an outcome. A witness has seen and experienced things that can help determine motives. Many servants of the Lord have opened doors for us. In every generation, there have been difference makers. Our job is to cast aside the things that make running difficult. Each of us has a course that has already been established.

When hurdlers enter a race, they expect to clear hurdles while they run. God has warned us that our race is an obstacle course. Our race is not one where getting to the finish line first is important. Our race is about continuing to the finish line. A cheering section has been appointed for you. Their sacrifice should help us navigate confidently through an otherwise intimidating ordeal.

REFLECTION:

September 26

"Those who hate of the LORD would pretend obedience to Him, and their time of punishment would be forever" (Psalms 81:15 New American Standard).

This is a psalm of Asaph as he pondered the condition of his people. Sometimes in order to know how you got where you are, you must look back. We can still suffer from the decisions of yesterday. Asaph remembered how God pleaded with His people to follow Him. He also remembered how they disregarded God's plea. We don't generally recall how we ignored God on our way to this current calamity. If God led you where you are, you should have peace where you are. If God didn't lead you where you are, don't be surprised at the difficulty. Even if He didn't lead you there, He doesn't want to leave you there.

Children should never be mistaken for haters of the Lord. A hater of the Lord is simply someone who doesn't allow Him to guide them. We all have children that think they are grown before their time. God has more children like that than anyone else. If you don't want to follow God, don't pretend in your commitment. He still knows that your deception will seal your fate. Asaph just wanted the people of God to celebrate the establishing of the nation even if things aren't great right now.

REFLECTION:

_____

_____

_____

_____

_____

_____

_____

_____

_____

September 27

"Slaves, be obedient to those who are your masters according to the flesh, with fear and trembling, in the sincerity of your heart, as to Christ" (Ephesians 6:5 New American Standard).

This language is very difficult to understand since we live in a country where people basically do whatever they feel like doing. However, as Christians, we must operate with a different mindset. When I was in the Army, we were governed by the rules of the military. We were still under the laws of the land, but our primary obligation was to the codes we were sworn in under. Now as believers, we get our "marching orders" from our commanding officer. A bondservant (slave) is one that volunteers to be a servant to his master. We shouldn't be offended by the terms servant and master because we serve a Master that is kind and compassionate. Furthermore, He demonstrated everything He required from His followers.

Everyone in authority must recognize they are also under authority. The level God takes you to is dependent upon how you treat those under your authority. Paul's message in this verse is to the servants. When we serve those God assigns us to, we are representing Him. Even Jesus submitted to authority knowing He would one day answer to the Father. If Jesus placed Himself under human authority for a time, why would any of us think we don't need to submit?

REFLECTION:

_____

_____

_____

_____

_____

_____

_____

_____

September 28

"Cease striving and know that I am God; I will be exalted among the nations, I will be exalted in the earth" (Psalms 46:10 New American Standard).

I believe this psalm was written in the midst of a great deal of turmoil. The psalmist talks about things going on around him. The elements that caught his attention were "natural" things. He discussed the earth, the waters, the seas, the mountains, and even the wars that ravage the earth. Although all of these events are real, the fact remains that God is still on the throne. He is still the magistrate in charge of everything. Sometimes I see my own circumstances like the unsettled waters and seas that seem to be doing their own thing.

God declares in other parts of His word that He determines the borders of the waters. He tells the oceans how far to go and doesn't worry about whether or not they will heed His command. Other translations use the words "be still and know." God's determined outcome is that He will be exalted among the nations and in the earth. Authorities and servants alike will speak of Him when it's all settled. Waters, mountains, seas and oceans may seem awesome and even intimidating, but God will be remembered after everything else is forgotten.

REFLECTION:

September 29

"Though it is the smallest of all your seeds, yet when it grows, it is the largest of garden plants and becomes a tree, so that the birds of the air come and perch in its branches" (Matthew 13:32 Niew International Version).

Jesus taught parables that revealed kingdom truth to those for whom it was intended. He showed how the kingdom of heaven is relative to a grain of mustard seed. You need spiritual discernment to understand the value and potential in something that wouldn't catch your eye. The mustard seed was the smallest seed, but it outperformed all other seeds in comparison to it. Your faith may be small right now, but because God's potential exists in that faith seed, it can grow beyond your wildest dreams.

God wants your growth to be so profound that others will find refuge in it. God has fashioned the body of Christ in such a way that we benefit from the faith of one another. We are an interdependent force that houses the Spirit of God Himself! This parable of the kingdom was designed to prevent us from despising small beginnings. What lasting difference does it make if a large seed produces a small harvest? It is much more miraculous when a small seed produces a large harvest. People may overlook you now, but when God matures you, they will find rest in your strength.

REFLECTION:

September 30

"And they were saying to the woman, 'It is no longer not because of what you said that we believe, for we have heard for ourselves and know that this One indeed the Savior of the world'" (John 4:42 New American Standard)

It is a wonderful thing that this woman of Samaria traded in her sordid reputation in order to testify of Christ. It is more wonderful when someone decides to investigate for themselves. No matter what anyone says, you must have your own encounter with Jesus. I still believe the woman was valuable because she gave a focus to their expectation. Every Jew that has ever lived has been told of a Messiah that will establish the kingdom of God. Throughout the ages, there was an anticipation of the One to come.

Can you imagine how many times there have been rumors of the Messiah? Many great people have aroused the curiosity of those waiting for Him. But now, they have investigated the claim. They have tasted and seen. They have confirmed the internal witness. They have met Immanuel! Out of all the people ever born, there is only one Savior. Ever since the days described in this verse, many have heard, and many have witnessed. When you have been truly changed, you will spread the news. You will spread it with your lips and spread it with your life. This is no time to be silent. He is the Savior of the World!

REFLECTION:

OCTOBER

October 1

"A double minded man [is] unstable in all his ways" (James 1:8 King James Version).

We have to look within in order to discover the root of double-minded behavior. Any time the life of a child of God is completely disconnected, it isn't anyone else's fault. Is it fear that causes double minded behavior? First, I believe a double-minded person is someone who can't even really determine what to believe. If you believe God is true, then stop following flattering orators that offer you nothing but brief good feelings.

The path of God is actually seldom comfortable, but it is always spiritually profitable. Since the way of God is infinitely higher than our ways, we can't possibly be walking with God if we're engulfed by instability. I often have to stop in my tracks and ask God for wisdom because I can't anticipate my next step. What you believe will either keep you in times of trouble, or it will fail you in times of trouble. Be of good cheer; God is able to keep you!

REFLECTION:

October 2

"For wicked and deceitful mouths are opened against me, speaking against me with lying tongues" (Psalms 109:2 English Standard Version).

David is pleading for the Lord to represent him. He asked the Lord in the first verse of this Psalm to not hold His peace. It can be very difficult to wait for the Lord to make a move. We must remember that God doesn't panic like we do. Actions may speak louder than words, but words have a lingering effect when actions have changed. The mouths of wicked people have spewed poison about you. They have actually attacked your integrity more than you have heard. If the things you have heard are bad, imagine the things you haven't heard! I must commend David for not taking matters into his own hands. We can become impatient and get involved in turning a situation into a catastrophe. What is the difference between the wicked and the deceitful? Wicked people are wicked on the surface and underneath the surface. Deceitful people pretend to be something else on the surface and are wicked underneath. God has great plans to silence the lies about you. We have to learn how to live down the lies without making them true.

REFLECTION:

289

October 3

"At that time Jesus declared, 'I thank You, Father, Lord of heaven and earth, that you have hidden these things from the wise and understanding and revealed them to little children'" (Matthew 11:25 English Standard Version).

Jesus had a distinct purpose for the way He instructed His disciples and for the way He challenged others to investigate Him. Because the disciples were chosen, He explained the hidden meanings of the parables. A parable attempts to familiarize us with another world by using examples from our world. When you know your purpose, you can begin to thank God when you see His plan in action. God decided to manifest Himself to "ordinary" people. Wisdom and prudence are certainly commendable virtues. However, sometimes people act as though those virtues entitle them to preferential treatment with God! We will never get closer to God because we're better than anyone else. If you get close to God, it is simply because He allowed you to do so. Jesus honored the Father for His plan. When you make an ordinary person feel important, God is glorified. An often-forgotten person won't understand the love of God because they haven't seen Him in their life. When you can sense God accepting you, it helps get you through the rejections you experience everywhere else.

REFLECTION:

October 4

"We are careful to be honorable before the Lord, but we also want everyone else to see that we are honorable" (II Corinthians 8:21 New Living Translation).

How many people do you know that make themselves accountable to people they don't have to? When you're in leadership, some of the things you do becomes everybody's business. Are financial reports only available to tithing members? Are business meetings held at the church open to those seekers trying to decide if they want to join? You shouldn't give just anybody a vote, but you should give anybody a voice. As a matter of fact, Paul was talking about financial integrity when he wrote this chapter.

One thing that everyone is concerned about is how the offerings are handled. What does the church plan to do with all that money? Yet, we don't mind throwing money away and throwing it at things we don't want to get personally involved with. No matter how often you have been deceived, every church isn't filled with crooks. Paul was deliberate in his attempt to be blameless. It takes a wise steward to toe the line between being honorable to men and maintaining the discretion necessary to know what to make known and what not to make known.

REFLECTION:

October 5

"It was for freedom that Christ set us free; therefore, keep standing firm and do not be subject again to a yoke of slavery" (Galatians 5:1 New American Standard).

The gospel is GOOD NEWS. The only time it can become bad news is when it is misunderstood. Quite frankly, if it ever becomes bad news, then it was never the gospel. Don't get bogged down with traditions, human expectations, unrealistic goals, and guilt complexes. Since Christ made you free, why would you be a slave to anyone except Him? The things you do must be driven by God; otherwise, you will fizzle out in a maze of frustration and bitterness. Many will disagree with my following statement: Christians, if your spouse isn't a believer and hasn't been for years, spend MORE time with them and less time at church! Unbelievers don't understand why you're choosing God and not them. Your quality time will be more attractive than any church service, and it will allow you to DISPLAY the love of God instead of REPLAYING the love for church. He that winneth souls is wise.

REFLECTION:

October 6

"This only have I found: God made mankind upright, but men have gone in search of many schemes" (Ecclesiastes 7:29 New International Version).

Mankind was made in the image of God. The power of choice is the greatest freedom any person can have. God had to give man the power to choose Him, or man could "create" an alternative. When a lust for something or someone else conceives, it gives birth to sin (James 1:15). You will constantly be tempted, but sin isn't "alive" until you yield to the temptation. God isn't the author of evil. He simply gave His creative prowess to others who used it to "create" evil. Since the original fall, man has found new creative ways to go against the original plan. Schemes are demonic in nature and can only lead to a web of destruction. We must be careful not to blame God for the way things are. Even though He knew the choices that would be made, He had to give us the right to choose.

REFLECTION:

October 7

"For this is what the Lord, the God of Israel, says, 'The jar of flour will not be used up, and the jug of oil will not run dry until the day the Lord gives rain on the land'" (I Kings 17:14 New International Version).

When you don't have enough to sustain your situation, can you make someone else's need a priority? This widow had already told the prophet that she was going to cook the last meal for herself and her son and then die. You will be challenged at times to see if you can give before you receive! You are ripe for a miracle when you look out for others before yourself. What did she have to lose? We will often hold on to things that won't last when God's will is to let Him hold it so it won't run out! When you give your last to God, He will make sure your resources remain until He sends other provisions. Don't be afraid; an open hand will open the door for God to bless you.

REFLECTION:

October 8

"And Abraham said to his young men, "Stay here with the donkey, and I and the lad will go yonder; and we will worship and return to you" (Genesis 22:5 New American Standard).

God told Abraham to offer Isaac for a sacrifice. Abraham told his servants that he and Isaac would return after a time of worship. Abraham waited his entire life for Isaac yet didn't hold back the "gift" from God. Everything God promised was wrapped up in Isaac. Isaac came from God, so why couldn't he be given to God? Worship is a very private matter that the Father controls. If you don't offer something, you're not worshipping! We cannot go empty-handed into the presence of God. The beauty is that God has already given you what you need to offer Him. Bring a broken heart and a contrite spirit, and God will meet you. A pure heart won't withhold the priceless treasure God demands. God always gives more than He receives. Whatever you bring to Him will return to you in greater measure.

REFLECTION:

October 9

"But He replied, 'It has been written, Man shall not live and be upheld and sustained by bread alone, but by every word that comes forth from the mouth of God'" (Matthew 4:4 Amplified Bible).

When you are at your weakest moment; hungry, tired, and tested, what is your reply? The word of God is light, living, strength, hope, perseverance, truth, correcting, sustaining, empowering, and ETERNAL!! Besides, the word is the only weapon the devil has to respect. You cannot resist him with any other battle instrument. He will even attack your praise. Your armor is defensive, yet His word is offensive. If you don't respond with what has already been written, you are on your way to defeat. No wonder Job said, "I have esteemed your word more than my necessary food!"

REFLECTION:

October 10

"So, Joshua subdued the whole region, including the hill country, the Negev, the western foothills and the mountain slopes, together with all their kings. He left no survivors. He totally destroyed all who breathed, just as the Lord, the God of Israel, had commanded" (Joshua 10:40 New International Version).

At first glance, this would seem awfully cruel. However, this destruction is a picture of what we must do with our carnal nature. The believer has three main enemies: the flesh, the world, and the devil. This war shows how each must be "killed." The hills and slopes portray the world that must be subdued. The Negev desert is like those fleshly remote areas in our lives, and the kings represent the devil who tries to take authority. There is no room for compromise, and God demands that we take equal action. In the Christian life, it's kill the flesh or be killed.

REFLECTION:

October 11

"Who is he that condemns? Christ Jesus, who died-more than that, who was raised to life-is at the right hand of God and is also interceding for us" (Romans 8:34 New International Version).

Let me go on record to say that if you know Jesus as your PERSONAL savior, please don't let your salvation be subject to anyone's discretion but God's! People will always try to make you "measure up" to their standards. There is too much scripture in your favor to allow such confusion. Why would Jesus intercede for someone who will only die and perish? That would be quite a waste. If we rely on our performance, His death is in vain because we can please God by keeping the law. He died because you CAN'T perform!! Don't misunderstand; we should love God enough to want to please Him. You weren't saved by works, so how can you be lost by them? Nobody misses going to heaven because of their conduct, only because He NEVER KNEW YOU! Write me if you have dialogue.

REFLECTION:

October 12

"Blessed is he that cometh in the name of the Lord: we have blessed you out of the house of the Lord" (Psalms 118:26 King James Version).

This is the same word the crowd cried when Jesus rode in on the donkey during his triumphal entry into Jerusalem. Amazing how the mouth will confess things the heart doesn't really believe. The Bible tells us there is a day coming when even the demons will bow their knee and confess with their tongue that Jesus is Lord, thereby glorifying God the Father. This is exactly why salvation starts with a conversion of the heart before a confession of the mouth. You can fool people with what you say, but God is listening to what's really inside of you! Jesus is indeed the blessed one whether we really believe it or not. He is the fulfillment of ALL that is glorious! He saves in the name of the Lord, heals in the name of the Lord, delivers in the name of the Lord, and even judges in the name of the Lord. The only way to be blessed is to be eternally related to the blessed ONE!

REFLECTION:

October 13

"For he hath made him to be sin for us, who knew no sin; that we might be made the righteousness of God in him" (II Corinthians 5:21 King James Version).

God is very passionate about His relationships. The fact that He could sacrifice His own Son for us is more than incredible. Nothing less than LOVE could cause Him to watch as Jesus was brutally mangled up to and including the crucifixion. Great love produced a great sacrifice, which produced a great anticipation of a great inheritance. There was actually a divine exchange of natures. Jesus took on our sin nature while He gave us His divine nature. When you know what really happened on the cross, it will help you understand what was intended for YOU! As the bumper sticker says, "Christians aren't perfect, just forgiven." Everything we get from God is free. It has to be free because you can't afford what it costs, and you can't earn what it provides.

REFLECTION:

October 14

"Therefore, let no one act as your judge in regard to food or drink or in respect to a festival or a new moon or a Sabbath day" (Colossians 2:16 New American Standard).

Many times in your life, someone will take it upon themselves to presume to know what's best for you. Paul had the status to tell the Colossians what to do if he wanted to but decided it is best to let them be free in Christ. Jesus died for you, and His death freed you from the bondage of others' expectations! You can eat what you want, celebrate what you want, observe what you want, and decline to observe whatever you want. It is nothing less than spiritual abuse for someone with a title or position to tell you that you have to be like them to please God. You have to be like Jesus to please God. If the Apostle Paul can understand this, surely we can too! God has given us all things richly to enjoy, so thank Him for all that you have and enjoy it richly.

REFLECTION:

October 15

"Hear; for I will speak of excellent things; and the opening of my lips shall be right things" (Proverbs 8:6 King James Version).

The plea of wisdom is, "HEAR ME!" When you examine your own life; how many things do you wish you could do over again? Or have you ever said: I wish I knew then what I know now? There is more to wisdom than mere experience. Wisdom will help you think in advance before you make an important decision. Wisdom will tell you to wait when your feelings tell you, "Why wait?" Wisdom will also tell you to get a second opinion sometimes. Since wisdom will speak things excellent and right, we should look and listen for it in life's corridors.

REFLECTION:

October 16

"I am weary of my life and loathe it! I will give free expression to my complaint; I will speak in the bitterness of my soul" (Job 10:1 Amplified Bible).

Job shared his feelings from his perspective. God doesn't mind if you "vent" as long as you don't accuse Him of unrighteousness. Circumstances have a way of wearing you out if you don't share your heart. We need to heal emotionally and spiritually the same way we would allow a broken bone to heal. God knows that we often can't see past our current position, so His ear is open to our voice. The difference is, God said that Job was an upright person that feared Him and avoided evil. Have you ever wondered what God is telling Satan about you?

REFLECTION:

October 17

"And the scripture, foreseeing that God would justify the Gentiles by faith, preached the gospel beforehand to Abraham, saying, "ALL THE NATIONS SHALL BE BLESSED IN YOU" (Galatians 3:8 New American Standard).

Many people have a problem with the Jews being God's chosen people. The scripture makes it clear that God chose Abraham before there were a chosen people. Abraham was from Ur of the Chaldees. Chaldeans were pagans. Before a nation can be born, an individual must be chosen. The promises were made to a man with godless roots, then God changed his name from Abram to Abraham. So actually, the gospel started with a Gentile, made him a father of the Jews, and then came back to the Gentiles. God always had a universal plan to reveal Himself to mankind. So, whether you are a natural child of Abraham through the flesh or an adopted child of Abraham through the Spirit, the gospel still makes him your father.

REFLECTION:

October 18

"Moreover, you shall not follow the customs of the nation which I shall drive out before you, for they did all these things, and therefore I have abhorred them (Leviticus 20:23 New American Standard).

God's plan has always been that His people would be noticeably different from everyone else. If you go shopping, don't you want to identify those who can help you? We should wear the "uniform" of Christlikeness so when anyone needs our assistance, they can identify us. American theology seems to be saying that we can get away with things others couldn't. Our success as a nation is a result of grace, not reward. God is no respecter of persons. He honors His WORD! God simply wants to make sure His ambassadors represent Him properly.

REFLECTION:

October 19

"All things are lawful unto me, but all things are not expedient: all things are lawful for me, but I will not be brought under the power of any" (I Corinthians 6:12 King James Version).

Paul's first statement of things being lawful unto him has to do with external things. The second statement of things being lawful for him has to do with internal things. We certainly have liberty to serve God, but He wants us to be careful not to revert to bondage. We were delivered from slavery, so why deliberately choose it? Corinth was an extremely gifted church that wasn't very mature. Our growth depends on our continued freedom. God doesn't want to continually release us from the enemy's prison just to use us!

REFLECTION:

October 20

"For as churning the milk produces butter, and as twisting the nose produces blood, so stirring up anger produces strife" (Proverbs 30:33 New International Version).

It seems like some people go through great efforts to stir up anger. We shouldn't be people who separate close friends or cause discord among brethren. If there is someone in your circle that can't resist gossip, you must guard your spirit against the poison that comes forth. Remember, evil communication corrupts good manners. You can't make butter from milk or cause a nosebleed by mistake. These are deliberate acts that come from evil plans. Our efforts should lead to edifying, not condemning.

REFLECTION:

October 21

"I am the God of Bethel, where you anointed a pillar, where you made a vow to Me; now arise, leave this land, and return to the land of your birth" (Genesis 31:13 New American Standard).

You have a very important part in the plan of God. If you're walking close to Him; expect a visitation. He will first remind you Who you're walking with. He will also cause you to remember when you wanted to commemorate the difference He made in your other predicaments. Next time you have an issue, call to remembrance how we walked you through the last one. We have made many promises to God, and He hasn't forgotten any of them. Arise and separate yourself from those who have no inheritance with you. It's impossible to live among those you can't walk with! God is in the process of bringing you to the promised land of your NEW birth. Don't get too distracted by things that are only temporary.

REFLECTION:

October 22

"Behold, I am going to send an angel before you to guard you along the way, and to bring you into the place which I have prepared" (Exodus 23:20 New American Standard).

Once you know God, you never have to worry about getting "lost" on your journey. You won't make it because you know how to get there; you won't make it because you picked up a map; you won't even make it because you see footsteps. You will make it because He will escort you safely home. Jesus said: "I go and prepare a place for you." It's a special place because it's not complete until YOU get there! Angels escort us even though we don't see them. Goodness and mercy follow us every day to make sure the door is closed behind us. You are being prepared to spend eternity in a place prepared for you. Just think, everything your pure heart desires will be there for you to richly enjoy. Praise God from whom ALL blessings flow!

REFLECTION:

October 23

"Now to Him Who, by (in consequence of) the [action of His] power that is at work within us, is able to [carry out His purpose and] do superabundantly, far over and above all that we [dare] ask or think-infinitely beyond our highest prayers, desires, thoughts, hopes or dreams" (Ephesians 3:20 Amplified Bible).

WOW! Why isn't this kind of ability at work in our circumstances? Apparently, the scope of God's involvement is determined by how well this power is changing US! If this power isn't transforming our lives into His image, giving us the strength to resist the devil, or showing us how to love your neighbor as yourself, why would God change the situation? God expects to change us, then we can change the environment. He told Adam and Eve to subdue the earth. The revelation is: he came from the earth, so he was really being commanded to subdue himself and then his environment. You already have the power at your disposal. If His power is dormant within, don't expect it to be superabundant without!

REFLECTION:

October 24

"Therefore, if any man be in Christ, he is a new creature: old things are passed away; behold, all things are become new" (II Corinthians 5:17 King James Version).

I once heard a dynamic definition of new which said, "Anything new means it has NO PAST!" What a wonderful act of grace where God can eliminate our past. That doesn't mean it never existed, but simply that it has no bearing anymore. I am no longer separated from God. I am no longer an enemy of God. I am no longer an object of wrath! Because I am in Christ, my sins are buried in Him along with my PAST. When God creates, He starts with nothing but His mind. I am fashioned in the Spirit according to the mind and will of God. Old things are deceased; new things are determined.

REFLECTION:

October 25

"For whatever is born of God overcomes the world; and this the victory that has overcome the world-our faith" (1 John 5:4 New American Standard).

This verse doesn't make victory optional. This is a declaration of a victory that has already been won! We overcame when Jesus overcame! The things you experience in life are mere setbacks. Stop calling them defeats! As far as God is concerned, it's already over. Jesus was slain before the foundation of the world, which means you were already safe before you got here. Faith doesn't mean you believe you will make it; Faith embraces what is hoped for and proves what isn't here yet. If your faith is in you, I am VERY concerned about you. We need the kind of faith that overcame the WORLD—not just my problems.

REFLECTION:

October 26

"Therefore, my beloved brethren, be ye steadfast, unmovable, always abounding in the work of the Lord, forasmuch as ye know that your labor is not in vain in the Lord" (I Corinthians 15:58 King James Version).

This last verse in chapter 15 begins with the word "therefore" because the preceding 57 verses established the faith. The chapter started by explaining the gospel message. Next, he talks about how we should conduct ourselves. Then, he taught the hope of the resurrection. Finally, we want to ABOUND in the work of the Lord. To abound means we should be increasing in favor with God. Our labor for God will not go unrewarded. The motivation to serve God starts with the fact that He saved us, continues in the fact that He keeps us, and culminates in the fact that He will RAISE us!

REFLECTION:

October 27

"For since the creation of the world, His invisible attributes, His eternal power and divine nature, have been clearly seen, being understood through what has been made, so that they are without excuse" (Romans 1:20 New American Standard).

I happen to be a revolutionary against the evolutionary. The only product produced by evolution has been the evolving ignorance of humanity! Man has become the wise fool and the intelligent ignoramus. In this 21st century that uses state-of-the art crime scene investigations, DNA expertise, and dental records, how come we can't look at the evidence and conclude that GOD IS? How often does the guilty party get apprehended at the scene? God may not be visible, but His "fingerprints" certainly are. God can be clearly seen and accepted by the overwhelming substantiation that points to His existence, His power, His wisdom, His majesty, and His care. Brainiacs have to learn to be satisfied with discovery without pretending to invent! Only God creates; we simply rearrange.

REFLECTION:

October 28

"Then my people will live in a peaceful habitation, And in secure dwellings and in undisturbed resting places" (Isaiah 32:18 New American Standard).

As you read this verse, the most logical question that comes to mind is, *WHEN?* A preceding verse tells us that this will be a reality when the Spirit of God is poured out from on high. A peaceful habitation is only possible when the Prince of peace is in charge. Right now, the only secure dwellings are either tightly locked, or heavily guarded. The people of God can look forward to the benefit of knowing that this godly "community" will consist of only those who have been transformed. An undisturbed resting place also means there will be no such thing as an emergency. Rest comes when work is done. May God teach us to anticipate that day; and help us to come as close as we can in the meantime.

REFLECTION:

October 29

"Do not work for the food which perishes, but for the food which endures to eternal life, which the Son of Man shall give to you, for on Him the Father, even God, has set His seal" (John 6:27 New American Standard).

A seal is a mark of authenticity, a stamp of approval, and an endorsement of power and authority. God wants us to know that ignoring Jesus is ignoring Him. Jesus wants to give you the soul satisfying food that will keep you. We understand the importance of natural food, but what about spiritual food? We even toil for the kinds of things that don't impress God. The bible makes comparisons to things we can relate to, so we won't excuse ourselves for using our own methods. God took the time to inspire His word, Jesus took the time to embody His word, and the Spirit took the time to explain His word. Now, YOU take the time to feed on His word. If not, your enemy has the time to feed on you.

REFLECTION:

October 30

"Let no man say when he is tempted, I am tempted of God: for God cannot be tempted with evil, neither tempteth he any man" (James 1:13 King James Version).

The human heart wants to blame another source for the magnitude of our inner struggle. This "warfare" should prove to us that we were truly born in sin and shaped in iniquity. Without God we could do nothing good, so how could He be the author of temptation? God certainly can test you to allow you to see yourself. No one would ever say that the tests you take in school caused you to fail. It is unthinkable to say that life wants you to fail. God isn't your enemy! Life certainly has many pitfalls, but the temptations come from the dark areas of your soul that respond to the bait presented by the prince of darkness. God dwells "above" everything, and anything evil cannot ascend to His domain. Certainly then, evil couldn't possibly descend from His domain.

REFLECTION:

October 31

"No, I neither have let my mouth sin by cursing my enemy nor by praying that he might die" (Job 31:30 Amplified Bible).

Even though Job wasn't listening to the conversation God had with Satan concerning him, he obviously knew that an "enemy" was at work in his situation. God allows the enemy to bring out the best in us. Your trials have been tailored to illuminate the God in you. No one else can endure what you endure. Only God knows what has been placed in you. I know you think you can't go on, but you MUST! Remember, God is at the end of every road, and we shall give account to Him. No amount of suffering will justify giving Him an excuse. The only way to be exempt is if you're sinless and die an innocent death on a cross. Any takers?

REFLECTION:

NOVEMBER

November 1

"You, dear children, are from God and have overcome them, because the one who is in you is greater than the one who is in the world" (I John 4:4 New International Version).

Did you notice the first word in this verse? "YOU!" Yes you, the one everyone counted out, the one that wasn't supposed to amount to anything, the D student, the one who was the brunt of all the jokes, the latest in a long line of dysfunctional misfits, the juvenile delinquent, and the one at the bottom of the barrel! Guess what? When God looks for someone to use, He typically starts at the bottom of that same barrel! Now you are a DEAR child. Now you have a resource of strength that even the devil(s) can't defeat. If you don't defeat yourself, you can't lose. People don't know your worth because they can't see deep into the treasury of your heart. You are from God, for God, in God, by God, with God, and to God, so praise God because He made you on purpose for His purpose!

REFLECTION:

_____

_____

_____

_____

_____

_____

_____

_____

_____

_____

_____

_____

_____

_____

November 2

"When you go to war against your enemies and see horses and chariots and an army greater than yours, do not be afraid of them, because the Lord your God, who brought you up out of Egypt, will be with you" (Deuteronomy 20:1 New International Version).

The warfare we face today is primarily in our minds. This verse uses words that might compare to seeing an enemy who is stronger, faster, and has us out-numbered. The things we imagine can cause great defeat. Yet the One we believe can assure us great victory. God is with you! Saving you from the "Egypt" of sin was the hardest thing God will ever have to do for you. Cast down anything from your mind that doesn't agree with His word, and you will not be afraid.

REFLECTION:

November 3

"Whoever observes the [king's] command will experience no harm, and a wise man's mind will know both when and what to do" (Ecclesiastes 8:5 Amplified Bible).

There is no safer place than the protection of the King. Safety is found in obedience. Strict adherence to the word of God will keep the hedge around you. God says, "If you love Me, keep My commandments." It doesn't matter how much you pray, fast, consecrate, dance, or speak in tongues if you're rebellious. To obey is better than sacrifice. When you want to please God, He will direct your path. Wisdom is realizing that God is at the beginning and the end of every decision. He will tell you what to do and when.

REFLECTION:

November 4

"For by thee I have run through a troop; and by my God have I leaped over a wall" (Psalms 18:29 King James Version).

God has afforded His people tremendous favor. One of the greatest aspects of His favor is the fact that you are UNSTOPPABLE! David understood how God was responsible for his victories. Even if you're a military genius, you still need God's protection. It takes great confidence in God to run toward a troop—much less run through it. God even helps you over the walls in your life that were unscalable. When you acknowledge God, He gives you much more to ponder. Your life is full of opportunities to bless the Lord. Time after time, He has proven to be a marvelous influence in your life. Morning by morning new mercies come your way. You don't have to find them; they find you. How can we not serve a God like this?

REFLECTION:

November 5

"He who overcomes shall inherit these things, and I will be his God, and he will be my son" (Revelation 21:7 New American Standard).

If you want to overcome, you have to be familiar with adversity. No one asks for trouble, but trouble always asks for a chance at you! Allow your situation to be an opportunity for the glory of God to shine in you. This is much easier said than done. Since you will encounter trouble anyway, why not let God have His way? He overcame every resistant force so you could be empowered to RISE! The things you stand to inherit are much better than the things you go through. God says He will belong to you, and you will belong to Him! You will inherit everything John saw in his vision: New Jerusalem and all of its splendor. Everything your heart can imagine will be greatly exceeded. It is well worth giving up what this life has to offer for what you will gain in the next one.

REFLECTION:

November 6

"Because He has fixed a day in which He will judge the world in righteousness through a man whom He has appointed, having furnished proof to all men by raising Him from the dead" (Acts 17:31 New American Standard).

So, the debate continues. Is Jesus the one or not? Well, all other wanna-be's are still used-to-be's buried in their graves. No one else has defeated the ultimate enemy: DEATH! In the approximately 2000 years since Jesus died, God remains undefeated in all attempts to disprove the resurrection. When it's all said and done, you will have to answer to the One God has appointed. Let the debate continue—God hasn't changed His mind. The day is still coming, regardless of who believes it. Would you want to chance being wrong?

REFLECTION:

November 7

"They who are willfully contrary in heart are extremely disgusting and shamefully vile in the eyes of the Lord, but such as are blameless and whole-hearted in their ways are His delight" (Proverbs 11:20 Amplified Bible).

God has no plan or sacrifice for those who are deliberately stubborn and rebellious. Even in the Old Testament, there was no offering you could bring for a deliberate act. You could only pay restitution. God says rebellion is like witchcraft and stubbornness is idolatry. Rebellion means you go opposite of your instruction. Stubbornness means you refuse to move in the right direction. Either way, God is sickened by this kind of mindset. HOWEVER, when we walk with Him and willingly submit to His leadership, He delights in us. Blameless doesn't mean perfect; it means above reproach. To be wholehearted, we have to surrender our lordship to His Lordship.

REFLECTION:

November 8

"What I am saying is that as long as the heir is a child, he is no different from a slave, although he owns the whole estate" (Galatians 4:1 New International Version).

This is another striking contrast between law and grace. When we were slaves to the law, it was impossible to benefit from the "estate" of grace. Furthermore, someone has to die in order for the assets of an estate to be distributed to the heirs. The Galatians were considering retreating to the slavery of trying to keep the law when in fact, to do so was IMPOSSIBLE! The people of God have to be forgiven in order to mature to the point of receiving the blessings. The Father has adopted us to bring us into the reality of His inheritance. God has chosen you! If you are His child, you own everything because He owns you, and He owns everything. Stop walking around like a pauper and recognize your unlimited potential. You can only reach what has been set before you. With faith, you can embrace your future by believing it in the present.

REFLECTION:

November 9

"Watch yourself that you make no covenant with the inhabitants of the land into which you are going, lest it become a snare in your midst" (Exodus 34:12 New American Standard).

It's truly amazing how easy it is to fall into traps after deliverance comes. We often pray for God to deliver us and grant us prosperity, health, and longevity. However, few of us make plans for what happens after He answers those prayers! One way to hasten the blessings of God is to have a plan for when He moves. God wanted His people to avoid the traps of idleness in freedom. It's not hard to figure out what to do when you're a slave. A snare is something that hooks you. A hook always causes a tearing of the flesh in order to be freed. The plan of God is to spare us the damage that snares cause. If we watch ourselves, we can walk in foresight instead of always learning from hindsight.

REFLECTION:

November 10

"For even the Son of Man did not come to be served, but to serve, and to give his life a ransom for many" (Mark 10:45 New International Version).

The earthly mission of Jesus was one of serving the will of God to bring many sons and daughters to glory. We often get confused about what positions really mean. We must work and serve before we can be served. The leader is the "chief servant." If the Son of Man put your needs before His own, why can't we put the needs of others before our own? We are often too entangled by petty pitfalls and can't serve anyone. You won't rise in God until you fall in humility. Your redemption was so expensive, only Jesus had what it costs! He gave His all for you to get God's all. This verse came after the arguments about who would be the greatest in heaven. There will only be a great ONE in heaven. Sorry, but it won't be you! God gets all the glory because He deserves it.

REFLECTION:

November 11

"Do not say, 'I'll pay you back for this wrong!' Wait for the Lord, and he will deliver you" (Proverbs 20:22 New International Version).

Emotions, tendencies, adrenaline, and many other factors can easily cause us to take matters into our own hands. Too many of us haven't learned to take burdens and offenses to God, so He is left with no choice but to watch us work things out. Unfortunately, when we get through "working," we're no further ahead. What does it mean to wait? It seems to mean that we shouldn't be busy with something we can't improve anyway! God hasn't hired any holy vigilantes to make sure we carry out a contract of retribution. Even when things are wrong, it is GOD'S business to pay back. To wait for the Lord also means that you are keeping His commandments so He can work on your behalf. How can He fight FOR you if He has to constantly fight WITH you? It will be His pleasure to deliver you when you are operating in your place.

REFLECTION:

November 12

"For you know the grace of our Lord Jesus Christ, that though He was rich, yet for your sakes He became poor, so that you through His poverty might become rich" (II Corinthians 8:9 New International Version).

The sacrifice of Christ isn't usually mentioned as an example for Christians to downsize in exchange for someone else's upsize. As much as we claim to love Christ, I have yet to hear anyone who exchanged their riches for poverty in this day and age. Jesus owned EVERYTHING and gave it all up for us. We owned NOTHING and came to inherit everything. The door to true riches was locked until Jesus was given the key through His death. To be spiritually rich means you are thankful for the things you have in store for you. I'm glad this isn't all there is. It truly does get much better than this for the child of God.

REFLECTION:

November 13

"And at the end of the days I Nebuchadnezzar lifted up mine eyes unto heaven, and mine understanding returned unto me, and I blessed the Most High, and I praised and honoured him that liveth forever, whose dominion is an everlasting dominion, and his kingdom is from generation to generation" (Daniel 4:34 King James Version).

A sovereign met THE sovereign. The king had absolute power on earth, but God has absolute power in the heaven that controls earth. A humbling experience is usually what it takes to open our eyes, particularly when we are in charge. Some people are still dealing with the insanity that keeps them from seeking, recognizing, blessing, praising, and honoring God. He is God and had control long before you got whatever power you have. Our influence will be over soon. His influence is from generation to generation. He is worthy of all the tribute you can give Him. You shouldn't have to lose your mind to find it.

REFLECTION:

November 14

"And I have filled him with the spirit of God, in wisdom, and in understanding, and in knowledge, and in all manner of workmanship" (Exodus 31:3 King James Version).

This verse speaks of Bezaleel, the grandson of Hur, who helped hold up the hands of Moses for victory in the battle. The verse says nothing about Bezaleel speaking in tongues because he was filled with the spirit. The Spirit of God goes about the business of empowering workmen for the glory of God. Ephesians tells us that we are His workmanship created unto good works. Notice before we do ANYTHING, we must have wisdom, understanding, and knowledge. Then, and only then, can we be workmen for the Lord. Also, get this–Bezaleel was from the tribe of Judah, which means praise. When praise holds up your hands in the battle, you too can expect VICTORY!

REFLECTION:

November 15

"Do all things without grumbling and fault-finding and complaining [against God] and questioning and doubting [among yourselves]" (Philippians 2:14 Amplified Bible).

God knows He orders our steps, so it is good counsel for us to see everything from God's vantage point. If Paul could have this attitude from a prison, why can't we have it from a job? Or a warm home? Or a comfortable car? Or at a dinner table? Or in our king-sized bed? God gives us all things richly to enjoy. He is the giver of every good and perfect gift. He prepares your table in front of your enemies. He blesses and rewards you openly! Surely, we can accept His will by simply getting along with one another. Even our enemies shouldn't have to worry about us seeking revenge. We all MUST be healing agents in the family of God.

REFLECTION:

November 16

"How priceless is your unfailing love! Both high and low among men find refuge in the shadow of your wings" (Psalms 36:7 New International Version).

There is great consolation in knowing that God loves YOU. Your life will force you to examine and question love. The bible says there is no greater love than laying down your life for your friend. Unfailing love means no matter what you've done, God's love can be counted. He doesn't love the wrong things we do, but He loves us through them. It doesn't matter where you were; it only matters where you're headed. Everybody needs God, and we are all on the same level. A shadow is proof that something or someone is present. The presence of God is enough to provide the confidence in a place of refuge.

REFLECTION:

November 17

"For the day of the Lord draws near on all the nations. As you have done, it will be done to you. Your dealings will return on your own head" (Obadiah v15 New American Standard).

It should be abundantly clear that God reigns supreme in all the earth. When God makes a decree, nations and individuals must answer accordingly. With God, what each one does affects everyone, and what everyone does affects each one. Nations will answer for forgetting their sovereign creator. God keeps flawless records, and He will remember the things His enemies forget. As children of God, we don't have to tremble as this day draws closer. Our task is to warn those who haven't taken refuge in Jesus. God is merciful and gives many opportunities to avoid the fate of His opponents. He's coming back, even though many don't believe it.

REFLECTION:

November 18

"Wherefore come out from among them, and be ye separate, saith the Lord, and touch not the unclean thing; and I will receive you" (II Corinthians 6:17 King James Version).

One thing that has always been an expectation of God is that His people bear a distinction. God is not common, so His people cannot be common. God is not ordinary, so His people cannot be ordinary. Whenever there is a large gathering of ANY kind, it shouldn't take long to begin identifying differences in the crowd. Don't be ashamed, they will talk about you now but look for you later. The things you suffer are not because of who you are; you suffer because of who you follow. Don't just stand out in the crowd; stand out FROM the crowd. When He receives you, all that He has comes with Him.

REFLECTION:

November 19

"Having put him to sleep on her lap, she called a man to shave off the seven braids of his hair, and so began to subdue him. And his strength left him" (Judges 16:19 New International Version).

This is the tragic sunset on the life of Samson. Once an invincible man of God, he is now reduced to an object of ridicule and sport. No matter how strong and anointed one may be, they must still be careful not to trust strangers to the valuables locked in their calling. Samson knew what his mission was, yet he "trifled" with how it should come to pass. Can you ever become comfortable enough to fall asleep in the lap of your enemy? Unfortunately, it is as easy for you as it was for Samson. God considers His investment in you as priceless, yet many of us consider it worthless! We have sold our anointing for pleasure, habits, other people, fame, fortune, opportunity, and the prestige of reputation. Somehow God still finds a way to get His "money's" worth out of us. Where would you be without His forgiveness? Think about that when your offender needs your forgiveness as well.

REFLECTION:

November 20

"But of the tree of the knowledge of good and evil, thou shalt not eat of it, for in the day that thou eatest thereof thou shalt surely die" (Genesis 2:17 King James Version).

Well, there you have it. The reason behind mankind's failure: A pretty and coveted piece of fruit. Don't get mad at Adam and Eve because you would have done the exact same thing. There is something about the human heart that wants what it can't have. However, you CAN have it, just not the way you want it. Did you ever wonder what other trees were in the garden? Is there a tree of motives? A tree of thoughts? How about a tree of wisdom? The bottom line is the only way to get what God has is through OBEDIENCE! There aren't any shortcuts. God demands nothing less, deserves nothing less, and will settle for nothing less. He has already paved the way, just follow the footprints.

REFLECTION:

November 21

"Jesus answered her, if you had only known and had recognized God's gift, and Who this is that is saying to you, Give Me a drink, you would have asked Him instead and He would have given you living water" (John 4:10 Amplified Bible).

Jesus is in conversation with a Samaritan woman in the middle of the day, which goes against everything in the Jewish culture. The heart of God is always to reveal Himself at the greatest point of need. He isn't concerned about us being "traditional" enemies. If your soul is thirsty, He wants to quench your thirst. All you have to do is ASK! God gives of Himself constantly for the purpose of having a relationship with you. You are the perfect opportunity for Him to express love. Your part is to ask, seek, and knock. His part is to answer, reveal, and open.

REFLECTION:

November 22

"Do you not know that your body is a temple of the Holy Spirit, who is in you, whom you have received from God? You are not your own" (I Corinthians 6:19 New International Version).

Sometimes our actions tell a different story than our lips. God has chosen to "localize" Himself in a living temple that we call a BODY! It's amazing to think that an infinite God would actually dwell somewhere. David was astounded to know that heaven itself can't contain God, but He would confine Himself in a manner of speaking. Christ died for us; the Spirit dwells in us. We received the Spirit from God. Each member of the Godhead is intimately involved in your ownership. We have been thoroughly and completely paid for: in FULL! We cannot throw garbage around God's house and think there won't be consequences when the Landlord surveys His property. Be a living sacrifice and let God show His pleasure with the gift of a long and healthy life.

REFLECTION:

November 23

"And Sarah said, 'God has made laughter for me; everyone who hears will laugh with me'" (Genesis 21:6 New American Standard).

Sometimes people laugh at you when they think your life is past the point of productivity. You know things like, "You're too old for the job. You don't have a degree. You don't have the experience. You didn't go to a seminary, or YOU'RE JUST NOT WHAT WE'RE LOOKING FOR!" Well, God doesn't operate the same way. If you can just believe Him; you're just what He's looking for. Things you can't accomplish naturally can be done with regularity spiritually. Isaac's name meant laughter. Not the kind of laughter associated with ridicule, but the kind that causes you to shake your head in amazement. Sarah is best remembered for giving birth to Isaac, even though she had plenty of other admirable qualities. Get a good grasp on what's in store for you here because your life can't end without it!

REFLECTION:

November 24

"Beloved, I pray that you may prosper in every way and [that your body] may keep well, even as [I know] your soul keeps well and prospers" (III John v2 Amplified Bible).

John is impassioned to pray for the new leaders in the gospel. As a seasoned Elder, John understands that younger ministers and teachers need the support and encouragement of the older trailblazers. Many of today's leaders want to continue carrying the torch far too long. John's prayer focuses on the kind of prosperity that will pay heavenly dividends. If our bodies break down, what does it matter how much money we have? Your soul is part of your inner man, which gets renewed every day by the word (if you spend quality time in the word). It takes a good attitude to be able to mentor someone else after God has used you on the front lines. John knows that he can still have an impact for Christ in a way that coincides with his age. May we all take a lesson from him.

REFLECTION:

November 25

"Now there was a long war between the house of Saul and the house of David, and David grew steadily stronger, but the house of Saul grew weaker continually" (II Samuel 3:1 New American Standard).

Despite constant resistance, the plan of God for your life will come to pass. David wasn't the greatest father, the greatest husband, or even someone you would allow to teach anything other than a worship seminar. HOWEVER, it doesn't matter what you think of the one God has chosen. Romans says, "The ones He predestined, He called, and He justified, and He glorified." HE did it! God didn't pause to get your input about His choice! Glorified? But how can this be when we're not glorified in this life? Well, God doesn't see you in this life. God sees you AFTER this life, already seated in heavenly places. God isn't "tripping" about the things we choose to focus on. There is a long war between your flesh and your spirit. If you're God's child, it may take a long time, but your spirit will grow steadily stronger while your flesh gets continually weaker.

REFLECTION:

November 26

"Let the morning bring me word of your unfailing love, for I have put my trust in you. Show me the way I should go, for to you I lift up my soul" (Psalms 143:8 New International Version).

The morning has great significance in the outlook of an entire day. The morning marks the arriva of a new mercy. Sleep allows you to either turn the page on a night of enduring weeping or dream about the glow of a memorable day. Either way the morning presents the dawn of another opportunity to capitalize on the blessing of a new day. The first person you should say "good morning" to is God. After all, He said it to you when He brought you back into this dimension. The message of God's love awaits you every day. The birds whisper it; the sunrise declares it. The breeze carries it, and your spirit shouts it! When He has your attention, He will show you the way to walk, talk, live, and love. Lift up your soul to Him because He is the "GOOD" in good morning!

REFLECTION:

_____

_____

_____

_____

_____

_____

_____

_____

_____

_____

_____

November 27

"Take heed, brethren, lest there be in any of you an evil heart of unbelief, in departing from the living God" (Hebrews 3:12 King James Version).

The trials of life can cause us to wonder if God has forgotten that we belong to Him. Take heed simply means to make sure we understand the BIGGER picture. What God is doing in your life is always BIGGER than what's happening right now. If you're His child, there is a reservation for you in heaven. Nothing can prevent that. Your heart MUST always be assured that a BIG God has BIG plans for a BIG reunion. If you're not His child, why not? Ask Him to forgive your sins and save you. In fact, do it right now.

REFLECTION:

November 28

"For in him we live, and move, and have our being; as certain also of your own poets have said, For we are also his offspring" (Acts 17:28 King James Version).

The Apostle Paul spoke this message at Mars hill while explaining who the Greeks referred to as "the unknown God." The Greek culture has always been famous for philosophy and wisdom. However, when it comes to God, you cannot simply "know" Him through human logic. God must reveal Himself to you. He is revealed externally in nature and internally in your soul. There is an eternal part of you that can't be fulfilled unless He fulfills it. Paul preached Jesus because He is the answer to any human question, and the solution to any human problem. Yes, we are all His offspring, but you need a spiritual relationship to be His child.

REFLECTION:

November 29

"And the word of God increased; and the number of disciples multiplied in Jerusalem greatly; and a great company of the priests were obedient to the faith" (Acts 6:7 King James Version).

God always manifests His pleasure when things are done for the good of the multitude. Deacons were chosen because many were being neglected, as the apostles couldn't do everything or be everywhere. When leaders delegate, many more lives are touched. Make sure you're secure before you step into a ministry role. Insecurity can destroy a move of God. The job of the apostles was to stay in the word of God and prayer. Think of how many people would have been hurt if the leadership was on an ego trip! I won't speak for you, but I would hate to be following a leader who isn't studying and praying. Because of delegation, the word spread, converts joined, and even priests were compelled to renewed obedience.

REFLECTION:

November 30

"You believe that God is one; you do well. So do the demons believe, and shudder [in terror and horror such as make a man's hair stand on end and contract the surface of his skir]" (James 2:19 Amplified Bible).

Today's watered-down version of Christianity seeks to unify everyone into a jar of *anything-goes* acceptance. The book of James slaps us in the face with practical truth designed to make us examine ourselves. Just because you believe in the God of the universe, doesn't mean you KNOW Him! Demons don't glorify God. Your life should manifest a connection with Him in the works you do. In the above verse, terror speaks of the inevitability of doom while horror speaks of the defeat in confrontation. The enemies of God have nothing to look forward to now or later. We have to serve God on His terms, not ours. Make sure your belief isn't just surface facts but deep TRUTH!

REFLECTION:

DECEMBER

December 1

"For God so loved the world, that he gave his only begotten Son, that whosoever believeth in him should not perish, but have everlasting life" (John 3:16 King James Version).

This is probably the most popular verse in the entire Bible. However, examine it closely. God "so loved." God is love, which means everything He does is love motivated. Love not demonstrated is infatuation. Love not conceived is fantasy. Love with no object is frustration. Love without freedom is bondage. Love without heart is an obligation. Love without thought is duty. Love without care is abuse. Love without control is anxiety. Love without reciprocation is dangerous. Love without God is IMPOSSIBLE! God's love without a response is condemning. He gave His best to have a relationship with us, which gives Him the right to refuse to be ignored. You can't know God without Jesus, no matter what you call Him.

REFLECTION:

December 2

"He went up to the temple of the Lord with the men of Judah, the people of Jerusalem, the priests and the prophets-all the people from the least to the greatest. He read in their hearing all the words of the Book of the Covenant, which had been found in the temple of the Lord" (II Kings 23:2 New International Version).

This verse tells the deeds of godly king Josiah, who walked in the ways of the Lord. It's a shame when the word gets lost in the temple. Josiah knew the only way to bring about revival in God's people was through the Word. He took prophets, priests, men, EVERYBODY! All people need the word. Why didn't the prophets speak the word? Why weren't the priests ministering for the Lord? We tend to put off reading and hearing the word when things are going well. Be careful that the word doesn't get lost in your temple. "Thy word have I hid in mine heart that I might not sin against thee."

REFLECTION:

December 3

"But now abide faith, hope, love, these three; but the greatest of these is love" (I Corinthians 13:13 New American Standard).

This verse describes probably the greatest three components of the human spirit. Faith, hope, and love will outlast the physical body. They will leave an impression for you long after your voice is no longer heard. Faith can move mountains, faith can claim the invisible, and faith can embrace the impossible. Hope can endure hardship, hope can keep you on course for the promise, and hope can see the next morning in a nighttime of affliction. But love can be multiplied to change the recipient. Love can be felt by another; love is content to be empty as long as someone else is full. Faith and hope have accompanying feelings while love only needs an object to love. GOD IS LOVE!

REFLECTION:

December 4

"For we have not an high priest which cannot be touched with the feeling of our infirmities; but was in all points tempted like as we are, yet without sin" (Hebrews 4:15 King James Version).

We often feel like an island of tribulation. Our problems are so unique, who could possibly understand? This verse should be a strong consolation for all of us. Jesus was tempted in all areas. You are only tempted in your areas. Whatever you're going through, He is the perfect candidate for understanding. Correction: He is the ONLY candidate for understanding. He is tired of being the last resort. He has more time for you than anyone else and more solutions than anyone else. When it comes to your burdens, either He's carrying them or you are.

REFLECTION:

December 5

"Keep back thy servant also from presumptuous sins; let them not have dominion over me: then shall I be upright, and I shall be innocent from the great transgression" (Psalms 19:13 King James Version).

The judgment of God doesn't always move like lightning; it can be more like molasses. God is long-suffering so we have opportunity to repent. The psalmist knew that presumption is probably the biggest hindrance to fellowship with God. Just like Adam died immediately spiritually, when he ate the fruit, we suffer immediately spiritually when we operate in presumption. Our hearts are deceitful and desperately wicked beyond our own comprehension. The flesh wants to have DOMINION over us. Every believer's prayer should be, "Keep me from presumptuous sins, thereby preserving my innocence.'

REFLECTION:

December 6

"I am the Lord: that is my name: and my glory will I not give to another, neither my praise to graven images" (Isaiah 42:8 King James Version).

God declares that He refuses to share what belongs to Him! He is a jealous God. He is very serious about what He owns. Everything God made should bring Him glory. Even things that aren't alive bring Him glory because we stand in awe at His workmanship. The mind of God made each person different from the beginning of time. No other person or thing can ever be compared to Him. God won't sit by quietly while His praise gets sabotaged by misguided allegiance. If anyone dares to compete for the glory and praise of God, they will have to deal with divine indignation. Remember; HE IS THE LORD!

REFLECTION:

December 7

"He who trusts in himself is a fool, but he who walks in wisdom is kept safe" (Proverbs 28:26 New International Version).

Knowledge is information, but wisdom is the best application of knowledge in your situation. How can you trust in yourself when you aren't the source of anything? A wise person will know that there is someone above them, someone before them, someone besides them, and someone beyond them that has control. The only thing we have control over is how we respond to what life attempts to teach us. The fear of the Lord is the beginning of wisdom. A healthy reverence for God will keep you safe through the pitfalls of life. Your life will still hurt sometimes, but God will reveal purpose in the pain! Can anyone else do that? How can I lean on myself when I'm the one that needs help?

REFLECTION:

December 8

"You number and record my wanderings; put my tears into Your bottle; are they not in Your book?" (Psalms 56:8 Amplified Bible).

One aspect of God's love that is seldom talked about is His compassion. Think about it. God has every emotion you have, yet it is expressed in perfection. God can relate so well that He keeps your tears on record. Sometimes tears of joy, sometimes tears of pain. Your life can make a difference in heaven—live it accordingly.

REFLECTION:

December 9

"Remember this: Whoever sows sparingly will also reap sparingly, and whoever sows generously will also reap generously" (II Corinthians 9:6 New International Version).

I can feel your anxiety as some of you read this. Here we go again, another word about money. Well, even though this verse was pertaining to money, the principle is the same. In computer language the saying is: garbage in-garbage out. In recycling the term is: no deposit-no return. In the Bible, the term is: you reap what you sow. There's a song that says, "You can't beat God giving." I believe the song is true. However, God says He won't beat you giving either! He truly gives, but He gives according to your willingness to give. It may be time, belongings, care, concern, or even money. Rest assured, the harvest you're reaping now = the seed you planted then.

REFLECTION:

_____

_____

_____

_____

_____

_____

_____

_____

_____

_____

_____

_____

December 10

"The Lord your God has blessed you in all the work of your hands. He has watched over your journey through this vast desert. These forty years the Lord your God has been with you, and you have not lacked anything" (Deuteronomy 2:7 New International Version).

God has been the Lord of your life and your circumstances throughout your wilderness experience. Even though the desert has been vast, God is also Lord over the wilderness. He has blessed you despite intense heat, wild animals, disgruntled traveling companions, cold nights, and personal heartache. He hasn't done this from a distance; He has been WITH YOU! He carries provision for the journey. We often underestimate what's needed to make it in one piece, but God knows and all we have to do is ask, seek, and knock. God has enough resources for everyone in the world to be satisfied at the same time. He would still have plenty of leftovers regardless of the need. Truly, you have not lacked anything!

REFLECTION:

December 11

"But let him who boasts boast of this, that he understands and knows Me, that I am the Lord who exercises lovingkindness, justice, and righteousness on earth; for I delight in these things, declares the Lord" (Jeremiah 9:24 New American Standard).

The prophet Jeremiah wanted people to know that it's not about their wisdom, their might, or their riches. Usually when people want to boast, they boast about themselves or what they have accomplished. Rarely will you hear someone boast about what God has done for them unless you're in a testimony service. God takes great pride in His attributes. God takes great pleasure and delight when we acknowledge Him in our conversation. Everything you have is something you received. Where would you be if God forgot about you? What would you have if God didn't give? Don't forget where today's blessings come from because you will need Him again tomorrow.

REFLECTION:

December 12

"Men of Israel, listen to this: Jesus of Nazareth was a man accredited by God to you by miracles, wonders and signs, which God did among you through him, as you yourselves know" (Acts 2:22 New International Version).

The job of the preacher is to stir up the minds of the people to remember who Jesus is, what He's done, and how we benefit from His favor. Jesus doesn't do signs, wonders, and miracles to show off. We are people constantly in need of EVERYTHING He does. This verse uses an interesting word: accredited. You could say that God validated, co-signed, inhabited, endorsed, accepted, and confirmed the person of Christ throughout His earthly ministry. How often do we look for those who God has accredited? We live in a day where we give more credence to man's criteria than God's. When we represent God, He works through us for our good, His glory, and the edifying of the body.

REFLECTION:

December 13

"Above all things have intense and unfailing love for one another, for love covers a multitude of sins-forgives and disregards the offenses of others" (I Peter 4:8 Amplified Bible).

This is one of those verses that challenges the very fiber of your allegiance to Christ. I believe God is bringing someone to your mind that you really haven't forgiven, am I right? Well, if you expect to grow another inch in God, FORGIVE THEM! It will take intense and unfailing love. Love doesn't wear out. Sometimes we cover things, but we still see the lump under the blanket. We have trouble forgiving a single offense, let alone a multitude of sins. To disregard means the wound doesn't hurt anymore. Don't be afraid to let God work on you. After He did surgery on Adam, He closed up the flesh so well; you couldn't tell there was an operation. He can do the same for you.

REFLECTION:

December 14

"But now, by dying to what once bound us, we have been released from the law so that we serve in the new way of the Spirit, and not in the old way of the written code" (Romans 7:6 New International Version).

Laws are not written for the innocent but for the guilty. We were bound by the guidelines of what the law required until grace made us free. This doesn't mean that we are free to violate the character of God with no consequences. However, now we serve from a different perspective. We keep the law of the spirit from outside the prison bars instead of living out a death sentence. We were born guilty so the only way to be freed is through death: that is, the death of Christ. It is a tremendous thing to be completely forgiven. Jesus paid it ALL! When you understand just how much your ransom was, you won't take your service lightly. Your liberation is free but not cheap.

REFLECTION:

December 15

"And Moses sent to spy out Jazer, and they captured its villages and dispossessed the Amorites who were there" (Numbers 21:32 New American Standard).

The people of God can look forward to having everything that is meant for you to have. There are times when God simply wants to know how strong your faith is. The word Jazer comes from a root word in Hebrew that means: to help or succour; to surround. God allows you to see where your help comes from. Your help doesn't come from the ones occupying your territory. When your faith is properly aligned, you can defeat the world, the flesh, and confirm the defeat of the devil. Jesus already defeated Satan, so we just have to resist him. Nowhere does the Bible say to fight the devil. God has already fought that battle for you. The one that lives in you is the GREATEST! Since God is the earth's landlord, doesn't it make sense that His children uproot the enemy and occupy His territory?

REFLECTION:

December 16

"But now in Christ Jesus you who formerly were far off have been brought near by the blood of Christ" (Ephesians 2:13 New American Standard).

There is a tremendous significance in just being "near." When you're near someone, you have access to them. Being near carries a certain warmth. Being near enhances the connection you have with them. Being near gives you collective strength, resolve, and fellowship. Being near eliminates anxiety. Being near energizes hope. Being near helps you face the unknown. Being near defines unity. Being near embodies oneness. You can't have oneness when you're alone. Only God is complete all alone. It's impossible to be intimate and distant! The blood of Jesus is powerful because it brought us near to God. The shedding of His blood made it possible for our sins to be forgiven. God found a way to restore the image lost in the Garden of Eden. Now that you can be near, take a look for yourself and see the salvation that belongs to you.

REFLECTION:

December 17

"And God shall wipe away all tears from their eyes; and there shall be no more death, neither sorrow, nor crying, neither shall there be any more pain: for the former things are passed away" (Revelation 21:4 King James Version).

God will not literally "wipe" the tears from our eyes, but He will cause the "unremembrance" of the things that stimulate a sad response. Some tears come from a heart of joy, so those will not be done away with. Your "eyes" in this passage could very well mean "perspective." In the presence of God, you will be unable to accept another viewpoint. How God sees is how we will see. The absence of death, sorrow, crying, and pain proves that God didn't want it on earth either! Notice the distinction between tears and crying. Tears are the result of a temporary situation while crying is the result of a permanent condition. When God does a work, He leaves nothing undone. Not only does He fix the surface, He also heals the source!

REFLECTION:

367

December 18

"And when our enemies heard that their plot was known to us, and that God had frustrated their purpose, we all returned to the wall, everyone to his work" (Nehemiah 4:15 Amplified Bible).

Your enemy's sole purpose is to distract from the work that God has given you to do. The body of Christ needs more WORKERS and fewer spectators. God will motivate you from time to time by exposing the plan of the enemy. When life throws a curve at you, your job is to "return to the wall." The work of God must continue. God's job is to frustrate your hindering elements. God has given each of us a J-O-B, and it will require your entire life to complete it. We don't have time to fight battles that only God can win. He called Nehemiah to build walls, not to put out fires.

REFLECTION:

December 19

"Let the elders who perform the duties of their office well be considered doubly worthy of honor [and of adequate financial support], especially those who labor faithfully in preaching and teaching" (I Timothy 5:17 Amplified Bible).

Well, sometimes we need to remind the people of God that this is a job not everyone can do. Good Elders labor to make it easier for you. In the Bible, the terms Elder, Pastor, Overseer, Shepherd, and even Bishop have similar contexts. God loves the church so much that He provides "ministry gifts" to the body. You should only worship God, but please esteem those leaders that have proven themselves worthy. People don't mind the prosperity of businessmen, doctors, lawyers, athletes, musicians, actors, and other entertainers. What about religious leaders? I think those who serve God and His people sacrificially should benefit from their service. A good leader will make sure you benefit when they benefit. Obey the word and enjoy a fruitful life.

REFLECTION:

December 20

"Ye are my witnesses, saith the Lord, and my servant whom I have chosen: that ye may know and believe me, and understand that I am he: before me there was no God formed, neither shall there be after me" (Isaiah 43:10 King James Version).

This is God's message to the nations. There are many differences in cultures, communication, and concepts. However, God wants the world to know He has left a message on record. I AM GOD! He is the self-existent one. He is before the beginning and will be after the end. Many people find themselves searching for meaning, substance, and the answers to the question: why? This question has haunted us since we were first old enough to ask it. God has spoken, written, inspired, and actually lived the same message. God says, "I want to know you!" God has done all He will do to relate with you. Now, your job is to find Him in every aspect of your life. He's really there!

REFLECTION:

December 21

"For death is come up into our windows, and is entered into our palaces, to cut off the children from without, and the young men from the streets" (Jeremiah 9:21 King James Version).

Oh, that we could discern the times and tactics of the enemy. He has always tried to eliminate the young and sabotage the next generation. The people of God must be visible and influential. This verse perfectly describes the days in which we live. Men must minister to other men and young men! Where are the David-Jonathan relationships? Every gathering of believers must turn this crisis around before it reaches greater epidemic proportions. God's plan is the only plan that can assure survival through rampant chaos.

REFLECTION:

December 22

"For thus says the Lord of hosts, 'After glory he has sent me against the nations which plunder you, for he who touches you, touches the apple of His eye'" (Zechariah 2:8 New American Standard).

God is your protector, and He can only watch you suffer for a little while. The eye is the most sensitive part of the body, and the "apple" is another way of saying the pupil. God is extremely sensitive when it comes to His children. Another passage reminds us that He remembers we are only dust. We are helpless when it comes to defending ourselves against the enemy. The love He has for you will cause Him to respond to protect His glory! God can chastise you, but anyone else better watch themselves. That's why I like to say, "The next time the devil tells you you're not worth anything, ask him-why did God pay so much for me if I'm worthless?"

REFLECTION:

December 23

"And make straight paths for your feet, so that the limb which is lame may not be put out of joint, but rather be healed" (Hebrews 12:13 New American Standard).

The shortest distance between two points is still a straight line, even in the spirit. The love of God is unconditional, but His favor is very conditional. We must put "guardrails" around ourselves if we expect God to smile on us. The battle is between the flesh and the spirit. The one you feed the most will be the strongest. God has promised to LIGHT the path, but we must WALK the path. Life has a way of exposing those lame areas. If you choose to walk the straight and narrow way, your weaknesses will be healed.

REFLECTION:

December 24

"But the wisdom that comes from heaven is first of all pure; then peace-loving, considerate, submissive, full of mercy and good fruit, impartial and sincere" (James 3:17 New International Version).

There are two types of wisdom: wisdom from below, and wisdom from above. We don't usually consider counsel from devils wise, but the enemy actually has the best plan he can have. And, it has been working for ages! Fortunately, there is still a better plan. Wisdom from God is pure, meaning there are no hidden motives. Secondly, God's wisdom will pacify a potentially explosive situation. Thirdly, it doesn't require something you can't do. Fourthly, it will help you yield to what's right regardless of how you feel. Finally, the wisdom of God will not seek to repay a wrong and will cause the fruit of the Spirit to flow in your life. God speaks in every situation. We just have to be quiet long enough to hear and obey. Shhhhhhhhh!! I think I hear Him—don't you?

REFLECTION:

December 25

"For this day in the city of David there has been born for you a Savior, who is Christ the Lord (the Messiah)" (Luke 2:11 Amplified Bible).

The last thing I want to do is argue about what day Jesus was born on. The important thing is that HE WAS BORN! The announcement is clear: a Messiah, a Savior, has been born for YOU! This announcement is a worldwide, all-inclusive announcement. If you're a Jew, you're included. If you're a Gentile, you're included. Your race doesn't matter. Your gender doesn't matter, and your ethnicity doesn't matter. If you celebrate Kwanza, you still need a Savior. If you celebrate Hannukah, you still need a Savior. If you don't celebrate anything at all, you still need a Savior. God's love for you is demonstrated by providing an avenue to know Him. The world is divided as it relates to what the birth of Jesus means. It may not mean much to you, but it means everything to God! He laid down His life for the world! Regardless of what faith community you embrace, or what religious convictions you adhere to, there will be a day of reckoning. God says that Jesus is the only Way to God I choose to believe He was born for me, lived as my example, died for me, was raised from the dead to prove His authority, and will come back to claim me to live forever as His son. I will celebrate "THIS DAY" as the birthday of my Savior!

REFLECTION:

December 26

"For though by this time you ought to be teachers, you have need again for someone to teach you the elementary principles of the oracles of God, and you have come to need milk and not solid food" (Hebrews 5:12 New American Standard).

God knows what "grade" we should be in based on how long He has been revealing Himself. The trials in your life are equal to the time He has spent molding you. Sometimes we want to pretend we haven't been equipped to deal with any situation. If you don't pay attention to what is being taught on your current level, how will you glorify God on the next level? Maturity in Christ comes by passing tests, the same way it comes in your natural life. God doesn't offer scholarships. You have to go through successfully in order to be promoted. Milk is easily received and digested, but solid food must be cut into bite-sized portions. God deals with us according to what we SHOULD know, not where we are.

REFLECTION:

December 27

"For my thoughts are not your thoughts, neither are your ways my ways, saith the Lord" (Isaiah 55:8 King James Version).

This is a very popular verse of scripture. However, if we really understood it, we wouldn't question God as much as we do. How often do you actually ask God what He thinks about something? God wants to share His insights on everything you do. You won't always get crystal clear direction from the word. In these instances, God wants you to acknowledge Him so He can direct your path. Your answer won't always come through prayer and Bible study. Sometimes it will come through the dialogue you have with Him in a spontaneous situation. The ways of God are only understood through a close relationship with Him. You will need on-the-spot revelation at times. He doesn't always "prepare" you for everything like you want Him to. If you really trust Him, you will let Him lead you on short notice.

REFLECTION:

December 28

"And he shall reign over the house of Jacob forever; and of his kingdom there shall be no end" (Luke 1:33 King James Version).

This verse is part of the great announcement to Mary concerning her son Jesus. What I find particularly encouraging is how he will rule over the house of Jacob. If you recall, Jacob's name was actually changed to Israel, but he couldn't seem to act like his new name. Israel means prince with God. Jacob's fears kept him from completely enjoying his royalty. God has changed your name too, but sometimes we find ourselves living in fear. Too often it's our "condition" that hampers our real "position." God doesn't take back what He promised. We have the power and authority to choose to walk in the privileges or live beneath our privileges. God wants us to have fullness! Do you want what God wants for you?

REFLECTION:

December 29

"God has looked down from heaven upon the sons of men, to see if there is anyone who understands, who seeks after God" (Psalms 53:2 New American Standard).

You don't find God looking for a lot of things. But you will find Him looking for an opportunity to be gracious and merciful. Not only does He look down from a heavenly perspective, He also looks down the corridors of time for anyone who understands. Understand what? He is searching for those who understand the reason you were created, the will He has for your life, the hope you can have in an eternal future, the help you have in times of trouble, the ultimate outcome of sorrow, the personal touch of His ministry, and the doorway of access to Him. There's a thirst in your soul that only He can quench. There's a hunger in your soul that only He can satisfy. Seek Him and find real life!

REFLECTION:

December 30

"Keep yourselves in the love of God, looking for the mercy of our Lord Jesus Christ unto eternal life" (Jude v21 King James Version).

To keep yourself in the love of God doesn't imply some human effort to merit God's attention; this statement carries a meaning of your MINDSET. Keep your mind on the truth of God's love, so your conduct will be governed by your expectation. What should you expect? You should expect Jesus to reveal Himself either in your present situation or literally in bodily form! A child of God NEVER has to worry about the wrath of God. Yes, we get chastised, but that's an expression of love, not wrath. When you have made peace with God through Jesus Christ, His appearing will be one of extended mercy.

REFLECTION:

December 31

"Thou art worthy, O Lord, to receive glory and honour and power: for thou hast created all things and for thy pleasure they are and were created" (Revelation 4:11 King James Version).

What good is possessing everything if you have no one to share it with? God wants to share Himself with His creation. God created you for the purpose of getting glory. The heavens declare that there must be a GOD! I once heard someone say that believing in the big bang theory is like believing you can get a dictionary from an explosion in a printing shop. Creation is specifically ordered. You are fearfully and wonderfully MADE! You are the deliberate result of an intelligent plan. There is no other YOU! Never has been, never will be. Take time to find out what God had in mind by bringing you into existence. Go ahead and ask Him; He won't mind.

REFLECTION:

About the Author

Pastor Ray Henderson was born and raised in Buffalo, New York. He accepted Christ in 1984, received his ministry license in 1997, and was ordained in 1998. Answering the call to pastoral leadership in 2000, he has faithfully served in a variety of ministry roles over the years.

In 2012, Pastor Ray and his family relocated to Georgia. He went on to earn an associate's degree in theology in May 2016 and later that year, in September, founded Living Word Fellowship. His ministry is anchored in a passion for "*achieving spiritual maturity through biblical literacy.*"

Pastor Ray is joyfully married to Tiffany Patterson-Henderson. He is the proud father of Krystal Jeanette Henderson, who resides in Buffalo, NY. Pastor Ray and Tiffany currently reside in Locust Grove, Georgia, along with his mother-in-love Connie Dixon.

www.ingramcontent.com/pod-product-compliance
Lightning Source LLC
Chambersburg PA
CBHW062147080426
42734CB00010B/1589